CLACKAMAS COMMUNITY COLLEGE
LIBRARY
WITHDRAWN

500 GLASS OBJECTS

A Celebration of Functional & Sculptural Glass

D1441734

500 GLASS OBJECTS

A Celebration of Functional & Sculptural Glass

Introduction by
Maurine Littleton

LARK BOOKS

A Division of Sterling Publishing Co., Inc.

New York

Editor **Susan Kieffer**

Art Director **Stacey Budge**

Cover Designer **Barbara Zaretsky**

Associate Art Director **Shannon Yokeley**

Editorial Assistance **Delores Gosnell**
Dawn Dillingham

Art Production Assistant **Jeff Hamilton**

Editorial Interns **Kelly Johnson**
Megan McCarter
Meta Pry
David Squires
Sue Stigleman

Art Intern **Ardyce E. Alspach**

Proofreader **Rebecca Guthrie**

Cover and other image credits

Front Cover
JANET KELMAN
Fuchsia in Bloom, 2004

Back Cover
TOP LEFT **PAUL SCHWIEDER,**
Clear Lemon Bowl, 2004

BOTTOM LEFT **MARY VAN CLINE**
The Receding Nature of Time, 2000

RIGHT **KATE VOGEL &**
JOHN LITTLETON
Topsy Turvy, 2004

Spine
SONJA BLOMDAHL
B1401 Golden Blue/Amber/Lime, 2001

Page 2
DANTE MARIONI
Yellow Vessel Display, 2004

Title page
WENDY HANNAM
City Limit #3, 2003

Contents Page
PABLO SOTO
Red & Orange Silhouettes, 2004

Front Flap
STEVEN M. SIZELOVE
Gem, 2004

Back Flap
RICK MELBY
Polka Butt, 2004

Library of Congress Cataloging-in-Publication Data

500 glass objects : a celebration of functional & sculptural objects /
introduction by Maurine Littleton.— 1st ed.
    p. cm.
  Includes index.
  ISBN 1-57990-693-1 (pbk.)
  1. Glass craft. I. Littleton, Maurine. II. Title: Five hundred glass
objects.
TT298.A18 2006
748—dc22
                2005029989

10 9 8 7 6 5 4 3 2 1

First Edition

Published by Lark Books, A Division of
Sterling Publishing Co., Inc.
387 Park Avenue South, New York, N.Y. 10016

© 2006, Lark Books

Distributed in Canada by Sterling Publishing,
c/o Canadian Manda Group, 165 Dufferin Street
Toronto, Ontario, Canada M6K 3H6

Distributed in the United Kingdom by GMC Distribution Services, Castle Place, 166 High Street, Lewes, East Sussex,
England BN7 1XU

Distributed in Australia by Capricorn Link (Australia) Pty Ltd., P.O. Box 704, Windsor, NSW 2756 Australia

The works represented in this book are the original creations of the contributing artists. All artists retain copyright on
their individual works.

If you have questions or comments about this book, please contact:
Lark Books
67 Broadway
Asheville, NC 28801
(828) 253-0467

Manufactured in China

All rights reserved

ISBN 13: 978-1-57990-693-1
ISBN 10: 1-57990-693-1

For information about custom editions, special sales, premium and corporate purchases, please contact Sterling Special Sales
Department at 800-805-5489 or specialsales@sterlingpub.com.

CONTENTS

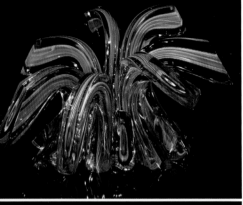

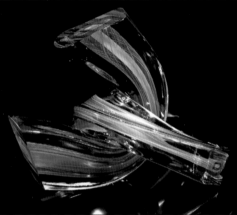

Introduction

For thousands of years, artisans have worked creatively with glass to various ends, from the utilitarian to the decorative. Only in the last 40 years, however, have a significant number of individual artists valued glass as a fine-art medium, exploring its unique properties and thereby developing its rich potential.

In the early 1960s my father, Harvey K. Littleton, introduced glassblowing into the art department curriculum at the University of Wisconsin in Madison. Today, a wide ange of glass programs are offered in art schools, universities, and craft workshops throughout North America, Europe, Australia, New Zealand, and Japan. Studio-glass artists from all of these regions are represented here in *500 Glass Objects* and include both emerging and established glassmakers. Rapid technical advances along with new aesthetic and conceptual approaches have further liberated glass and have made it a vehicle for personal artistic expression in works that are often quite dramatic or innovative.

Glass can be manipulated by myriad techniques. When melted in a furnace, glass can be blown, hot worked on a pipe, manipulated with tools, or cast by pouring it into any of several mold materials. Glass rods can be lampworked or flameworked over a gas and oxygen flame. In pâte de verre, powdered glass or small chips of glass are heated so that they can then be fused in a mold. Combining the forces of heat and gravity, sheets of glass can be slumped over a form and cooled to retain a shape. When glass is in its cold state, it can be sandblasted, acid etched, enameled, painted, ground, or cut. Additionally, glass can be glued or used in combination with metal, wood, and other materials, expanding its visual boundaries.

Some of the objects selected for this book display virtuoso technical skill, while others seem to be less-technically sophisticated but express considerable character. An apparent disregard for technique may be an aesthetic choice but, in fact, requires skills and knowledge only possible with years of experience—for example, *Slinky* by Jay Musler, shown here.

The qualities that artists can express utilizing glass are unlimited. Techniques can convey a variety of emotional states or ideas, play visual games with our perception, and can also emphasize aspects exclusive to this medium. Glass can appear to be fragile and ephemeral,

TOP
HARVEY K. LITTLETON
Ruby Spray, (14 parts), 1990
17¼ x 30 x 30 in. (43.9 x 76.2 x 76.2 cm)

CENTER
HARVEY K. LITTLETON
Blue/Lemon Linked Form, 1990
Linked: 12½ x 17 x 12 in. (31.8 x 43.2 x 30.5 cm)
Upright: 14 x 17 x 10½ in. 35.6 x 43.2 x 26.7 cm)

BOTTOM LEFT
JAY MUSLER
Slinky, 2003
8½ x 9 x 3½ in. (21.6 x 22.9 x 8.9 cm)

as evidenced by Janet Kelman's work in this collection, or it can be monumental, pristine and elegant, rough and crude, expressionistic and organic, or coolly calculated, hard-edged, and futuristic. The rough-surface treatment and thematic content can suggest an excavated artifact, as in William Morris' work, an example of which is shown here. Although it may be easy to classify glass works by technique, sources of inspiration are as diverse as the individual artist's personal vision.

Many of the glass objects in this juried collection reference specific artistic or decorative styles. For example, the influence of Italian artist Lino Tagliapietra is evident in some. Since the late '70s he has generously shared his knowledge and expertise in Venetian glass-working techniques, with its classically proportioned forms and often, bright colors. In other works the vessel surface serves as a canvas, as in Christian Schmidt and Cappy Thompson's work. A focal point for some of the artists here is the land, including the environment, and the relationship between humanity, nature, and the universe. Some artists evoke cultural traditions; others explore the human figure pictorially, or as a sculptural form; still others investigate formal aspects. But the overarching concern in this group is the truly celebratory use of color.

Because of the enthusiastic support of both private and corporate collectors, the marketplace for contemporary glass objects is now flourishing in such venues as art and craft fairs, retail stores, and galleries. There are even galleries that specialize exclusively in glass. To the delight of glass lovers everywhere, it is now common for museums to host exhibitions of contemporary glass. Dale Chihuly, the most celebrated artist working in glass today, has had more than 100 solo museum shows worldwide. Internationally recognized and respected museums such as the Metropolitan Museum of Art in New York City and the Victoria and Albert Museum in London have organized and catalogued important glass exhibitions, and a growing number of institutions have been the appreciative benefactors of large collections of contemporary glass donated to them, including the Toledo Museum of Art in Ohio, and the Carnegie Museum of Art in Pittsburgh, Pennsylvania.

As one views this body of work, one can't help but appreciate the tremendous diversity of these juried pieces, and brief mention here should be made about the manner in which the objects were chosen. Although initially we sought out contemporary bowls, vessels, and goblets in glass, we expanded the theme to incorporate nonfunctional works as well. The number of nonfunctional objects that refer to functional forms is thus a result of this change. The outcome is a dazzling display of bravura workmanship and a veritable rainbow of color for the viewer. I hope this view into the intriguing world of glass will both fascinate and inspire you.

—*Maurine Littleton*

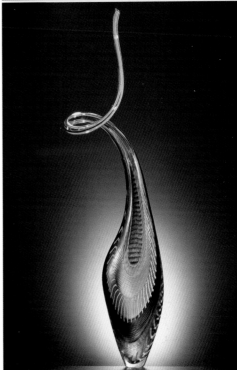

TOP
WILLIAM MORRIS
Artifact: Shard, 1993
16 x 25 x 8 in. (40.6 x 63.5 x 20.3 cm)
Photo by Rob Vinnedge

ABOVE
LINO TAGLIAPIETRA
Dinosaur, 2005
49½ x 14¼ in. (125.7 x 36.2 x 20.3 cm)
Photo by Russell Johnson

LISA SAMPHIRE
Lidded Bullseye Vessel, 2004

9½ x 12 inches (24.1 x 30.5 cm)
Blown triple incalmo, murrine
Photos by Vince Klassen

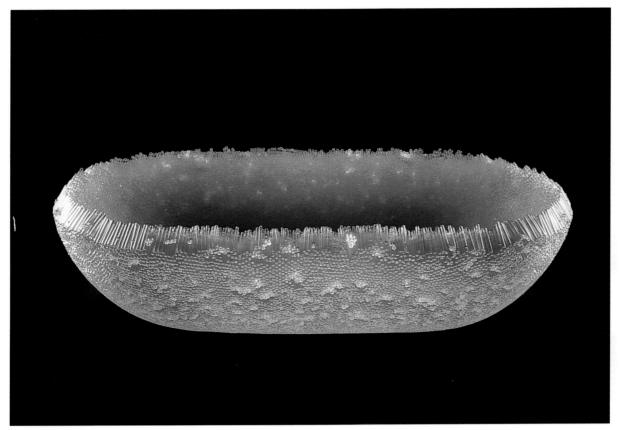

JULIUS WEILAND
Bath, 2004

8⅔ x 27⁹⁄₁₆ x 17¾ inches (22 x 70 x 45 cm)

Glass tubes; fused in a mold

Photo by Hanns Joosten

SUSAN J. LONGINI
Vase Analogy: Purple/Magenta, 2002

18 x 17 x 6 inches
(45.7 x 43.2 x 15.2 cm)

Pâte de verre glass, reservoir-cast
base; assembled

Photo by Pilchuck Glass School

NANCY KLIMLEY
Behind the Screens, 2004

13 x 6 x 6 inches
(33 x 15.2 x 15.2 cm)

Kiln-cast glass; lost-wax technique

Photo by Russell Johnson

This is a memorial to a pivotal family member who shaped my world and identity, and is now gone. Using the blown vessels as containers of memory, I attempted to capture lost moments and preserve the personal history of my family.

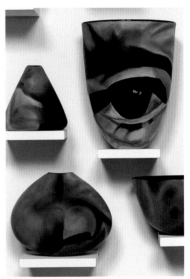

ANNETTE BLAIR
Keith, 2003

65¹⁵⁄₁₆ x 50 x 3¹⁵⁄₁₆ inches
(167.5 x 127.5 x 10 cm)

Blown glass, oil paint; sandblasted

Photos by Stuart Hay

NANCY CALLAN
Herringbone Top, 2005

11 x 14 x 12 inches (27.9 x 35.6 x 30.5 cm)

Blown glass; twisted cane

Photo by Rob Vinnedge

JEREMY LEPISTO
Symmetry of Suspense, 2003

4 x 35 x 1 inches (10.2 x 88.9 x 2.5 cm)

Kiln-formed glass

Photos by Paul Foster

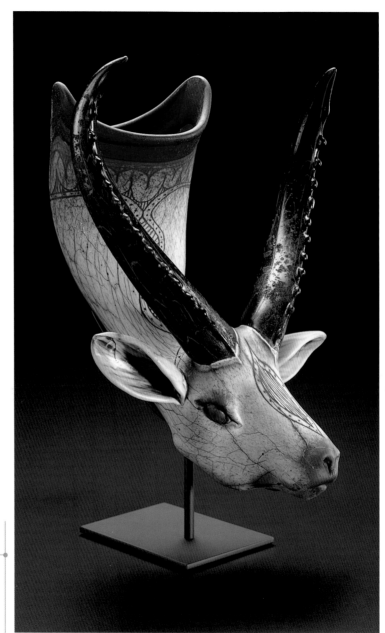

WILLIAM MORRIS
Lechwe Situla, 2000

18 x 13 x 13 inches
(45.7 x 33 x 33 cm)

Blown glass, steel stand;
sculpted

Photo by Rob Vinnedge

MARY VAN CLINE
Cycles of the Relationship of Time, 2003

25 x 26 x 6 inches (63.5 x 66 x 15.2 cm)

Photo-sensitive glass, pâte de verre, bronze patina

Photo by Rob Vinnedge

STEPHAN COX
Blue Bud with Red Tongues, 2005

12 x 11 x 11 inches (30.5 x 27.9 x 27.9 cm)

Hand-blown glass; segmented, carved,
cold fused

Photo by Don Pitlik

dave myrick
Neo-Tassa #1, 2003

8 x 7½ x 7½ inches (20.3 x 19.1 x 19.1 cm)

Blown glass; multi-layered, engraved, assembled

Photos by Tom Mills

MASAMI KODA
Seed, 2002

14½ x 15 x 9 inches (36.8 x 38.1 x 22.9 cm)

Lampworked glass, wood, copper rod, pipe, sheet, wire, silicon carbide

Photos by artist

This form is blasted right through to create a lace effect. The nature motif on this vessel suggests fertility and growth. Also included in the pattern is a beauty mark which signifies to me that she is proud of her fertility—adding to her power and strength.

CAROLYN PROWSE-FAINMEL
Beauty Mark, 2004

11¹³⁄₁₆ x 7¹⁴⁄₁₆ x 4¹⁵⁄₁₆ in.(30 x 20 x 12.5 cm)

Blown glass; sandblasted

Photos by artist

BRUCE PIZZICHILLO
DARI GORDON
Incalmo Sculptural Vessel, 2005

17 x 9 x 9 inches (43.2 x 22.9 x 22.9 cm)

Blown glass, wire; crackle technique, incalmo technique, carved, sandblasted, patinated

Photo by Lee Fatherree

JASON MORRISSEY
Set of Glass Spheres, 2003

Each: 2 x 1¾ inches (5.1 x 4.5 cm)

Blown, borosilicate glass; silver-fumed implosion

Photos by Robert Diamante

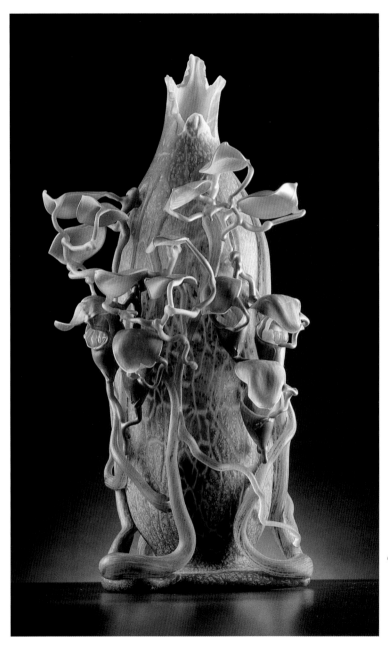

Each sculpture reveals its own story. In my imagination, I journey to a place where dark passages lead to splendid beauty. My sculptures are the discoveries— living, breathing creations that often take on human characteristics. These lines between nature, humankind, and fantasy have been blurred, and the deeper I explore, the more wondrous the world becomes.

VICTOR CHIARIZIA
Choosing the Path, 2004

17 x 9 x 9 inches (43.2 x 22.9 x 22.9 cm)

Blown borosilicate glass, enamels; lampworked, painted, sandblasted, acid etched, assembled

Photo by Tommy Olof Elder

GINNY RUFFNER
Studio Window, 2004

23 x 17 x 5 inches
(58.4 x 43.2 x 12.7 cm)

Glass, mixed media

Photo by Mike Seidl

JUDITH SCHAECHTER
Hemophilia, 2004

48 x 23 inches (121.9 x 58.4 cm)

Stained glass, copper foil; sandblasted,
engraved, enameled

Photo by Don Episcopo

Sixty-three individuals contributed text in twenty-two different languages, all of them addressing the experience of being from, or living in, Portland, Oregon. The central idea of *Portland Pamphlets* is that a work of art has to grow from the existing context of history, environment, and community. It becomes a coherent part of physical and social reality.

ZHAO SUIKANG
Portland Pamphlets, 1999

252 x 78 x 5 inches
(6.4 m x 3.8 m x 12.7 cm)

Slumped glass, fiber-optic lights; sandblasted, silkscreened

Photos by artist

27

SONJA BLOMDAHL
Golden Blue/Amber/Lime:
B1401, 2001

19 x 13 inches (48.3 x 33 cm)

Blown glass; multi-layered using
incalmo, battuto (etched)

Photo by Lynn Thompson

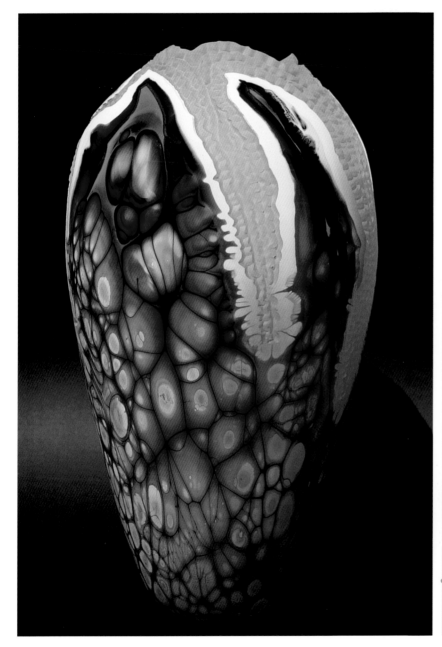

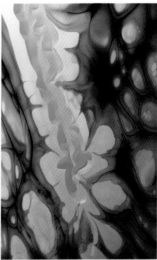

NOEL LAUE
Creation Vessel GCV17-SMC, 2001

18 x 9¾ x 9¾ inches (45.7 x 24.8 x 24.8 cm)

Blown glass; multiple overlays, sandblasted

Photos by artist

KATHERINE BERNSTEIN
WILLIAM BERNSTEIN
Face Goblets, 2002

6½ x 2¾ inches (16.5 x 7 cm)

Blown, hot-tooled glass; cane drawing

Photo by J. Littleton

KATHERINE BERNSTEIN
WILLIAM BERNSTEIN
Colored Face Goblets, 2002

7 x 3 x 3 inches
(17.8 x 7.6 x 7.6 cm)

Blown glass; cane drawing

Photo by J. Littleton

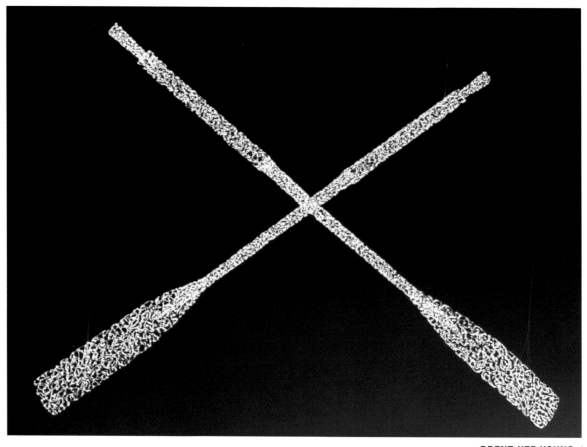

BRENT KEE YOUNG
Element Series: Pull, Earl!, 2003

94 x 9 x 2 inches (238.8 x 22.9 x 5.1 cm)

Flameworked, heat-resistant glass

Assisted by Yoshiko Asai
Photo by Dan Fox/Lumina

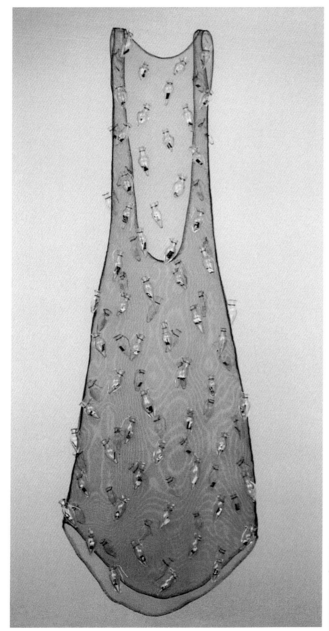

This dress hangs in space, holding a collection of moments in time and reflecting the journeys we take and what we take with us.

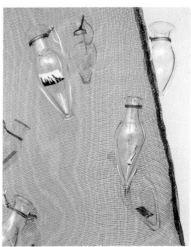

TANYA LYONS
Talebearer, 2004

72¹⁄₁₆ x 24⁷⁄₁₆ x 39³⁄₈ inches (183 x 62 x 100 cm)

Blown glass; photographs, copper, thread

Photos by artist

ELENA SHEPPA
Nuptual Cranes, 2005

4½ x 3 inches (11.4 x 7.6 cm)

Blown glass; two-color overlay, sandblasted, etched

Photo by George Johnson

MARY LYNN WHITE
Uranian Constellations II, 2005

9½ x 7¾ inches (24.1 x 19.7 cm)

Furnace-blown glass; encased
enamel painting

Photo by John Littleton

JOELLE LEVITT
Glow Wurm, 2004

15 x 16 x 3 inches (38.1 x 40.6 x 7.6 cm)

Blown and kiln-cast glass elements,
wood, fluorescent light, silhouette
cut-out

Photo by artist

MARY BAYARD WHITE
Corn from Katrina's Garden, 2004

14 x 9½ x 5 inches (35.6 x 22.9 x 12.7 cm)

Recycled window glass, bulls-eye glass;
cast, slumped

Photo by Esteban Salazar

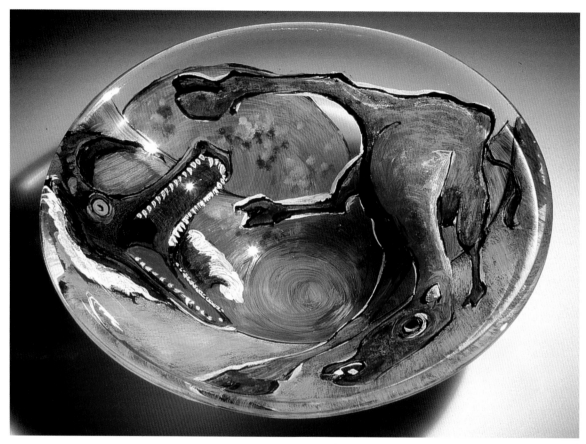

KARA van WYK
Camel & Crocodile, 2003

12 inches diameter (30.5 cm)
Blown glass; reverse painted
Photo by Wayne Torborg

KARA van WYK
Fox & Hen, 2003

10 inches diameter (25.4 cm)
Blown glass; reverse painted
Photo by Wayne Torborg

ELIZABETH COLEMAN
The Things They Carry, 2000

9½ x 3½ x 3½ inches each
(24.1 x 8.9 x 8.9 cm)

Lost-wax cast lead crystal;
electroplated, patinated

Photo by Bryan Heaton

JONG PIL PYUN
Eclipse IV, 2003

5 x 4 x 10½ inches (12 x 10 x 27 cm)
Borosilicate glass; lampworked
Photo by artist

JAMES MONGRAIN
Creature Series: Swan Goblet Set, 2000

11 x 2½ inches (27.9 x 6.4 cm)

Blown glass

Photo by Russell Johnson

MICHAEL MANGIAFICO
Black Spider, 2005

¾ x 3 x 2 inches (1.9 x 7.6 x 5 cm)

Moretti glass; torch worked, acid etched

Photo by Joelle Levitt

DONI HATZ
Blue-Claw Crab, 2004

3 x 10 x 7 inches (7.6 x 25.4 x 17.8 cm)

Blown borosilicate glass, colored glass
frit and powder; shaped

Photo by Mark Cheadle

45

JAMIE HARRIS
November Mod Installation, 2003

72 x 72 x 4 inches (1.8 x 1.8 x 10.2 cm)

Blown, carved glass

Photo by D. James Dee

CURTISS BROCK
Stone Vessel Grouping, 2000

Left: 18 x 12 inches (45.7 x 30.5 cm)
Middle: 14 x 14 inches (35.6 x 35.6 cm)
Right: 16 x 14 inches (40.6 x 35.6 cm)

Blown glass; cut, sandblasted,
acid etched

Photo by artist

CURTISS BROCK
Mosaic Vessels, 2001

Left: 22 x 12 inches (55.9 x 30.5 cm)
Right: 12 x 12 inches (30.5 x 30.5 cm)

Blown glass; sandblasted, acid etched

Photo by artist

ANJA ISPHORDING
#90, 2004

11 x 5⅛ inches (28 x 13 cm)

Kiln-cast glass; lost-wax technique, cut, polished

Photos by Ken Mayer

GABRIELE KÜSTNER
Glass Mosaic Plate, 2002

10¼ inches diameter (26 cm)

Painted glass cane; fused, slumped, cold worked

Photo by Maxwell

This piece is from a
series inspired by my
local landscape.

GARY BEECHAM
Appalachian Landscape, 2004

26 x 23½ x 5 inches
(66 x 59.7 x 12.7 cm)

Glass, stainless steel armature;
fused color-overlay rods

Photo by John Littleton

51

I enjoy using the domestic act of sewing to explore the complex expectations of women within the household.

SUSAN TAYLOR GLASGOW
Don't Forget, Pinkies Out Coffee Pot, 2004

13 x 10 x 7 inches (33 x 25.4 x 17.8 cm)

Fused and sewn glass; slumped, sandblasted photo imagery, glass enamel, waxed linen thread

Photos by artist

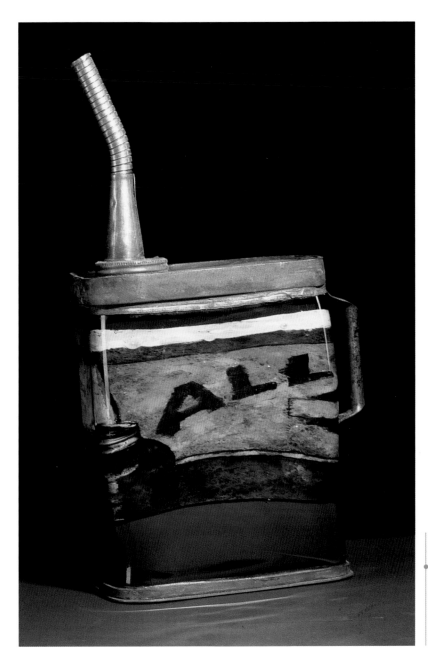

MAGAN STEVENS
Oil Can Series, 2000

19½ x 11½ x 6½ inches
(49.5 x 29.2 x 16.5 cm)

Blown glass, mixed media;
reverse painted

Photo by Pat Simone

MELISSA MISODA
Platform, 1999

16 x 5 x 3 inches (40.6 x 12.7 x 7.6 cm)

Blown glass, rubber, plate glass

Photo by artist

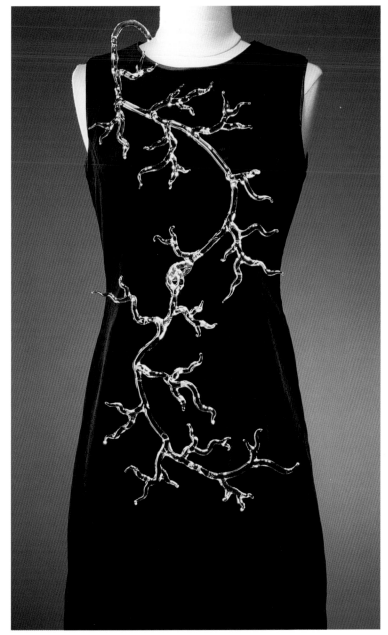

My wearable sculpture explores line and gesture. It reflects my fascination with sinuous Art Nouveau lines, tree branches silhouetted against the sky, icicles, and diagrams of old master paintings, where gesture can carry your eye through the painting.

BETH HYLEN
Branches, 2001

29¹⁵⁄₁₆ x 12 x 9¹⁄₁₆ inches
(76 x 30.5 x 23 cm)

Borosilicate glass, velvet dress; lampworked

Photo by Frank Borkowski

Discarded Dreams is about the hopes and dreams people put aside. The blue ampolina signifies the "dream" tossed along the side of the road of life. Like litter or debris on the side of the highway, foliage grows around the piece. The idea or dream is left behind, forgotten. This work was inspired by the different paths I've taken in my life, and the dreams I've discarded for other dreams.

MARC VandenBERG
Discarded Dreams, 2004

3½ x 5¾ x 3¾ inches
(8.9 x 14.6 x 9.5 cm)

Blown glass; lampworked

Photo by Leslie Patron

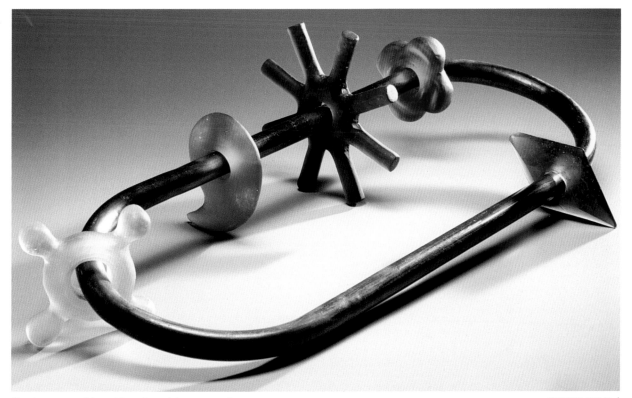

I'm interested in taking the object out of its normal context and materials.

BRENT COLE
Teething Ring, 2004

12 x 36 x 12 inches
(30.5 x 91.4 x 30.5 cm)

Cast glass, steel

Photo by artist

NANCY CALLAN
Classic Bee Buoy, 2005

15 x 11 x 11 inches
(38.1 x 27.9 x 27.9 cm)

Blown glass; incalmo technique

Photo by Rob Vinnedge

NANCY CALLAN
Bling-Bling Bee Buoy, 2005

18 x 13 x 13 in. (45.7 x 33 x 33 cm)

Blown glass; incalmo technique

Photo by Rob Vinnedge

LISA SAMPHIRE
Houdini Murrine Bottle, 2004

13½ x 6 inches (34.3 x 15.2 cm)

Blown incalmo with murrine; belted finish

Photo by Vince Klassen

CONCETTA MASON
Ignition, 1991

12½ x 8½ inches (31.8 x 21.6 cm)

Blown glass; controlled breaking, sandblasted

Photo by Henry J. Ponter

KENNY PIEPER
Primavera Bowls, 2002

Largest: 9 x 17 inches diameter (22.9 x 43.2 cm)
Blown glass; primavera and incalmo techniques
Photo by David Ramsey

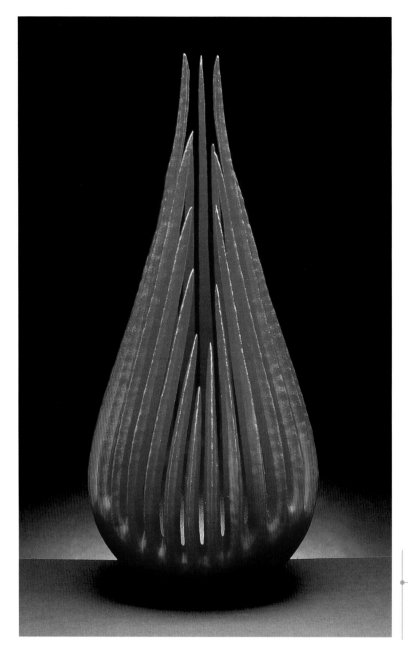

PAUL SCHWIEDER
Cadmium Drop, 2004

18 x 8 x 8 inches (45.7 x 20.3 x 20.3 cm)

Blown glass; sandblasted

Photo by Glenn Moody Photography

My work looks at balance and explores the relationship between opposites, presence and absence, surface and void.

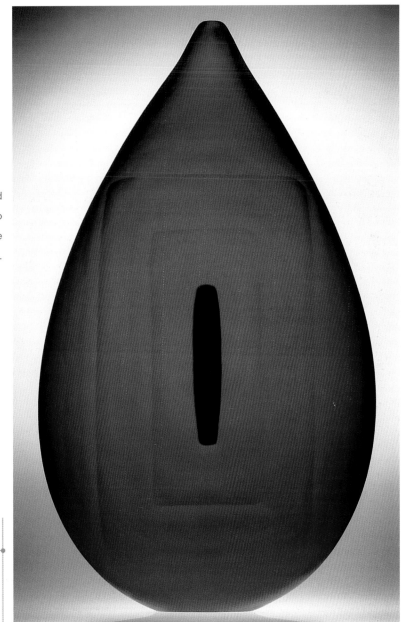

BENJAMIN SEWELL
Mound, 2004

16¹⁵⁄₁₆ x 9½ x 3½ inches
(43 x 24 x 9 cm)

Blown glass, black hot-glass inclusion; diamond-wheel cut

Photo by Larry Irvin

65

CYNTHIA MYERS
Cabernet Grapes, 1998

11 x 11 x 11 inches (27.9 x 27.9 x 27.9 cm)

Blown glass; multi-layered, sandblasted

Photo by Hap Sakwa

ANJA ISPHORDING
#70, 2002

9¼ x 10¼ inches (23 x 27 cm)

Kiln-cast glass; lost-wax technique,
cut, polished

Photo by Ken Mayer

Samarkand is an ancient Uzbek city
famed for its blue tile work. The large
deposits of lapis lazuli in the region
gave the ceramic tiles used for
architectural motifs their fantastic
blue glaze. Our *Samarkand* invokes
the luxuriant color and architectural
style of that city.

ANTHONY SCHAFERMEYER
CLAIRE KELLY
Samarkand, 2002

14 x 12 inches (35.6 x 30.5 cm)
Blown glass; carved canes
Photo by H&O Photography

NOEL LAUE
Creation Vessel GCV7-SDC, 2000

12 x 13 x 13 inches (30.5 x 33 x 33 cm)

Blown glass with multiple overlays; sandblasted

Photo by artist

KRISTON MICHAEL GENE
Carapace Vases #1, 2003

12 x 4½ inches each (30.5 x 11.4 cm)

Blown glass; engraved

Photo by artist

ELENA SHEPPA
Botanicals, 2004

7 x 3 inches (17.8 x 7.6 cm)

Blown glass; two-color overlay
sandblasted, etched

Photo by George Johnson

INITA ÉMANE
Memory Vein, 2003

24½ x 1⅕ inches (62 x 3 cm)

Fused glass, copper wire, glass enamel, bendet, glass pearls

Photo by Didzis Grodze

My intention was to make the entire form of *Memory Vein* quite simple, since the interplay of lines and the graphics create a sense of spatiality.

GARY BOLT
Celestial Sphere #3, 2004

6 x 9½ x 9½ inches (15.2 x 24.1 x 24.1 cm)

Sand-cast glass with multi-layered
inclusion; cut, ground, polished

Photo by Vince Klassen

This work was inspired by a story told by Deepak Chopra about the two goddesses in us all—wealth and knowledge. The mouth on one side forms a kiss, representing desires or what wealth can attain; the other side represents a state of contemplation, or knowledge. The story tells us to love them both, but to give our attention to knowledge; wealth will be jealous and follow wherever we go.

STEPHEN RICH NELSON
Silver Queen, 2000

32 x 10½ x 10 inches (81.3 x 26.7 x 25.4 cm)

Blown and hot-worked glass,
silver leaf; assembled

Photos by Walter Plotnick

This is one in a series of masks that explores psychological archetypes in a cultural context.

GILLIAN HANINGTON
Death Mask, 2004

11 x 5 x 2½ inches (27.9 x 12.7 x 6.4 cm)
Kiln-cast glass; carved granite base
Photo by artist

This piece is a contemporary search for classical form. The rich colors and faceted center element make this goblet unmistakably modern, while the shape pays homage to antiquity.

STEVEN M. SIZELOVE
Gem: Venetian Interpretation Goblet, 2004

9½ x 4 x 4 inches (24.1 x 10.2 x 10.2 cm)

Borosilicate glass; flameworked; blown, sculpted, cut

Photo by artist

RHONDA KOZAN
Ode to Urning, 2003

26 x 12 x 13 inches (66 x 30.5 x 33 cm)

Blown, sculpted glass, floral adhesive
paper, wood pedestal

Photo by artist

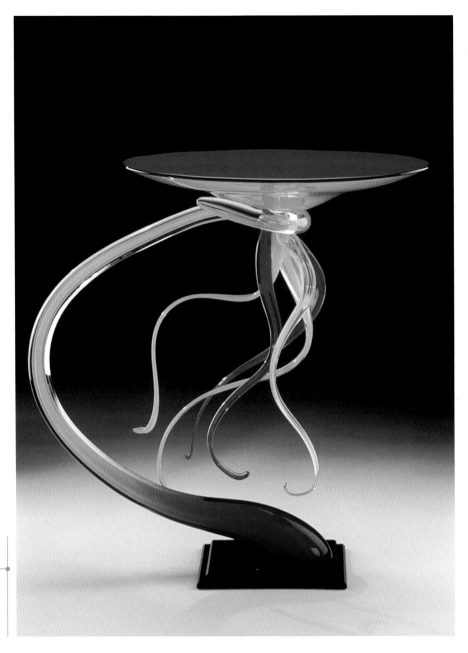

RANDY STRONG
Bonsai Bowl with Multi-Tails, 2004

29 x 22 x 20 inches (73.2 x 55.9 x 50.8 cm)

Blown glass; multiple layers
of color, cold fused

Photo by Keay Edwards

BONTRIDDER THIERRY
Untitled, 2004

19¼ x 27½ x 24 inches (49 x 70 x 61 cm)

Fused, thermo formed

Photos by Paul Louis

Traditionally, vases are made for utilitarian purposes. This piece strives towards analyzing other possible orientations and interpretations of a vase. Do vases have a hole? Is the vase silhouette necessarily exactly mirrored on the inside? Can horizontal or vertical planes describe volume?

SIDNEY HUTTER
120 Degrees of Three-Color Wheel Jerry Vision, 2004

16½ x 9½ x 9½ inches
(41.9 x 24.1 x 24.1 cm)

Plate glass; laminated, ground, polished

Photo by Charles Mayer

SIDNEY HUTTER
ABOVE LEFT

Vase with Yellow, Blue, Red, and Purple, 2004

16½ x 9½ x 9½ inches (41.9 x 24.1 x 24.1 cm)

Plate glass; laminated, ground, polished

Photo by Charles Mayer

ABOVE RIGHT

Three Views of Four-Color Wheel, 2002

16½ x 9½ x 9½ inches (41.9 x 24.1 x 24.1 cm)

Plate glass; laminated, ground, polished

Photo by Charles Mayer

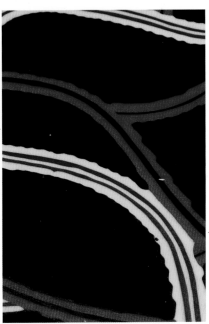

HELENA VAN NUYS
You Can't Get There From Here, 2004

15⅝ x 8¾ x 1½ inches (39.7 x 22.2 x 3.8 cm)

Fused glass; slumped, cold worked, sandblasted

Photos by Eva Heyd

DICK MARQUIS
Egg with Egg Cup #04-11, 2004

8¾ x 4¼ x 4¼ inches (22.2 x 10.8 x 10.8 cm)

Blown glass; granulare technique

Photo by artist

STEPHEN ROLFE POWELL
Nudging Lemon Scoop, 2004

28½ x 28½ x 21 inches
(72.4 x 72.4 x 53.3 cm)

Blown glass; murrini surface

Assisted by Chris Bohach, Jon Capps,
Matt Cummings, Paul Hugues,
Ted Jeckering

Photos by David Harpe

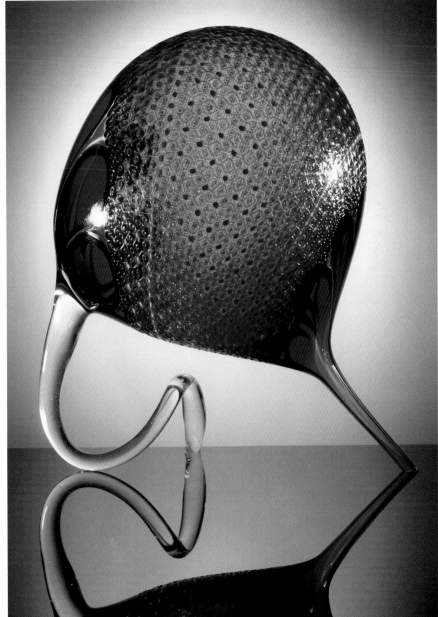

GEORGE BUCQUET
Peach-Opal Squash Blossom, 2004

11 x 15 x 15 inches (27.9 x 38.1 x 38.1 cm)

Hot-cast glass, copper, patina

Photo by Robin Robin

MARK SUDDUTH
Incalmo Canted, 2004

14 x 12 x 12 inches
(35.6 x 30.5 x 30.5 cm)

Hand-blown glass; cut, polished, engraved

Photo by artist

CHARLES PROVENZANO
Untitled, 2001

8 x 3½ inches (20.3 x 8.9 cm)

Blown glass; zanferico and overlayed transparent canes

Photo by Steven Berall

This work was inspired primarily by the poetry of William Butler Yeats, his interest in the tarot, and the esoteric medieval philosophy that is encountered in Spain and France. The sculpture is a color study based on the Three of Cups tarot card, which signifies fertility and abundance, and which, in this case, is starting to wane. It is a meditation on the transcience of beauty.

RENE CULLER
Three of Cups/ Past Prime, 2001

30 x 16½ x 16½ inches (76.2 x 41.9 x 41.9 cm)

Blown glass, pre-fused glass plate; cold worked, assembled, cast or kiln transformed, fused, slumped, pâte de verre

Photo by Robert Muller

This basket combines gesture and fluidity with a softness of color. It exemplifies the feeling that originally attracted me to glass.

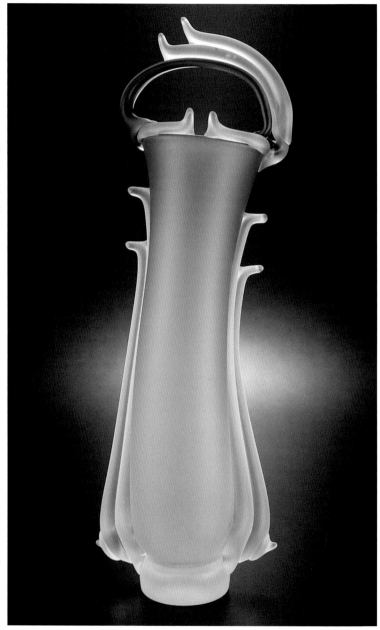

ROBERT LEVIN
Basket #132, 1999

18 x 6 x 4 inches (45.7 x 15.2 x 10.2 cm)

Blown glass; frosted, sandblasted, acid etched

Photo by artist

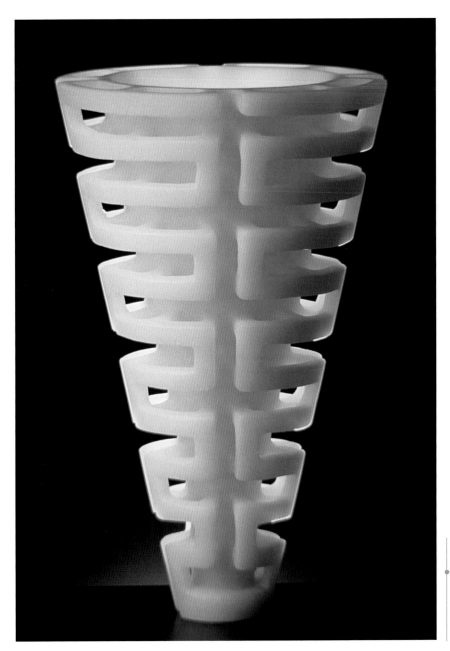

NANCY KLIMLEY
Lattice, 2003

7½ x 4¾ x 4¾ inches (19.1 x 12.1 x 12.1 cm)

Kiln-cast glass; lost-wax technique,
cage technique

Photo by Russell Johnson

The Greek myth of Pandora and the unleashing of the contents of the box entrusted to her inspired our *Pandora's Box*. As the story goes, hope was the last thing left in the box, and the box was closed before hope could be lost.

ANTHONY SCHAFERMEYER
CLAIRE KELLY
Pandora's Box, 2004

16 x 7 inches (40.6 x 17.8 cm)
Blown glass; carved cane
Photo by Jeff Shout

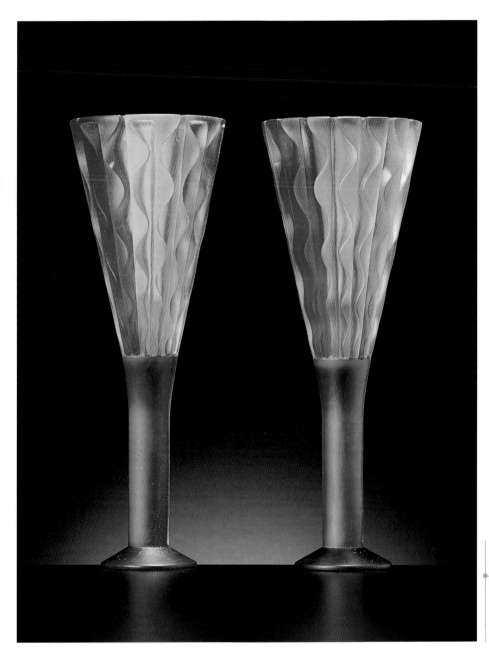

NANCY KLIMLEY
Indian Summer, 2004

13 x 4¾ x 4¾ inches each
(33 x 12.1 x 12.1 cm)

Kiln-cast glass; lost-wax technique

Photo by Russell Johnson

JUDITH SCHAECHTER
Specimens, 2004

25 x 37 inches (63.5 x 94 cm)

Stained glass, copper foil; sandblasted, engraved, enameled

Photo by Don Episcopo

My colorbar murrine series affords me the opportunity to experiment with color and fusing temperatures. *Summer Salsa* consists of approximately 700 hand cut murrine, eight colors of glass, and 60 color combinations.

ROBERT WIENER
Summer Salsa, 2004

15 x 15 x ¼ inches
(38.1 x 38.1 x 0.6 cm)

Fused glass; cold worked, slumped

Photos by Pete and Alison Duvall

DEBORA MOORE
Lady Slipper Kiko Bamboo, 2004

22 x 4½ x 5 inches (55.9 x 11.4 x 12.7 cm)

Blown, sculpted glass

Photo by Russell Johnson

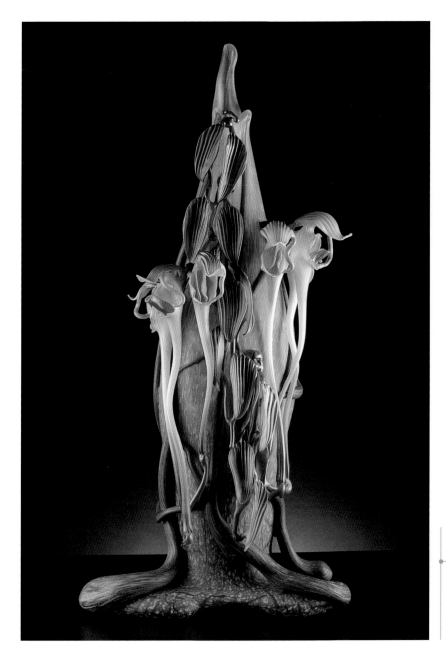

VICTOR CHIARIZIA
Gaia's Pleasures, 2004

18 x 8 x 7 inches (45.7 x 20.3 x 17.8 cm)

Blown borosilicate glass, enamels; lampworked, painted, sandblasted, acid etched, assembled

Photo by Tommy Olof Elder

97

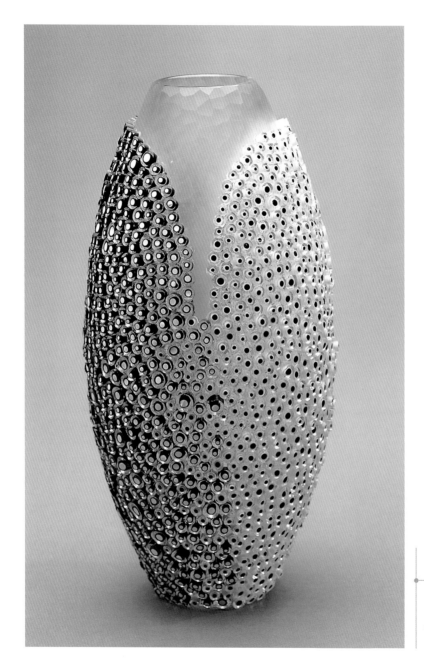

GABRIELE KÜSTNER
Untitled, 2003

10½ x 5¼ diameter inches (26.4 x 13.6 cm)

Blown glass, silicone-applied glass cane; cold worked, battuto ground

Photo by Maxwell

KAIT RHOADS
Jade, 2004

14½ x 9½ x 9½ inches (36.8 x 24.1 x 24.1 cm)

Blown glass; zanfirico cane, veiled murrine

Photo by Roger Schreiber

99

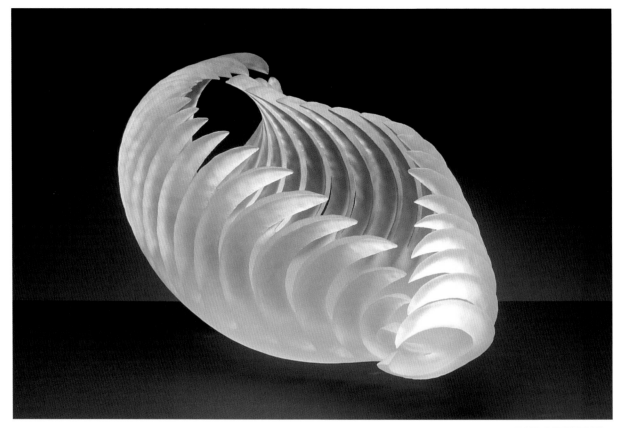

PAUL SCHWIEDER
Clear Lemon Bowl, 2004

5 x 19 x 7 inches (12.7 x 48.3 x 17.8 cm)

Blown glass; sandblasted

Photo by Glenn Moody

COLIN REID
#R1216, 2004

7½ x 17¾ x 12⅝ inches (19 x 45 x 32 cm)

Kiln-cast optical glass; gilded,
milled, ground, polished

Photos by artist

101

RENE CULLER
Nine of Cups, 2003

60 x 17½ x 17½ inches (152.4 x 44.5 x 44.5 cm)

Blown glass, pre-fused glass plate; Italian roll-up technique, pâte de verre, cold worked, assembled, cast or kiln transformed

Photos by Robert Muller

DEBRA MAY
Botanical Fire Bowl, 2004

10½ x 15 inches (26.7 x 38.1 cm)

Blown glass; sandblasted

Photo by Robin Stancliff

JACOB VINCENT
Spiral Tumblers, 2004

4 x 2½ x 2½ inches (10.2 x 6.4 x 6.4 cm)

Borosilicate glass; lampworked

Photos by Nash Studios

JAMES MONGRAIN
Opaque Yellow Goblet Set, 1999

11 x 2½ inches (27.9 x 6.4 cm)
Blown glass
Photo by Russell Johnson

JULIE GIBB
familial study #2, 2004

4⅓ x 8¼ x 2¾ inches (11 x 21 x 7 cm)

Blown glass; enameled

Photos by artist

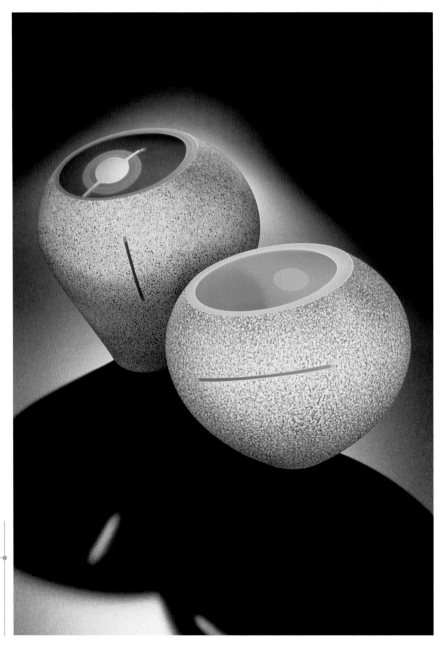

CURTISS BROCK
Stone Vessels, 2000

Left: 18 x 12 inches (45.7 x 30.5 cm)
Right: 14 x 14 inches (35.6 x 35.6 cm)

Blown glass; cut, sandblasted,
acid etched

Photo by artist

SONJA BLOMDAHL
Left: *Teal/Ruby B3402,* 2002
Right: *Topax/Aventurine Green B7002,* 2002

Left: 9½ x 10 inches (24.1 x 25.4 cm)
Right: 7½ x 8 1/2 inches (19.1 x 21.6 cm)

Blown glass; multi-latered incalmo,
battuto

Photo by Lynn Thompson

SHANE FERO
*A Bunch of Finches with
Assorted Berries,* 2005

Largest: 3 x 7½ x 2½ inches
(7.6 x 19 x 6.4 cm)

Flameworked glass; acid etched

Photo by John Littleton

ELENA SHEPPA
Predator/Prey, 2004

4½ x 3 inches (11.4 x 7.6 cm)

Blown glass; two-color overlay, sandblasted, etched

Photo by George Johnson

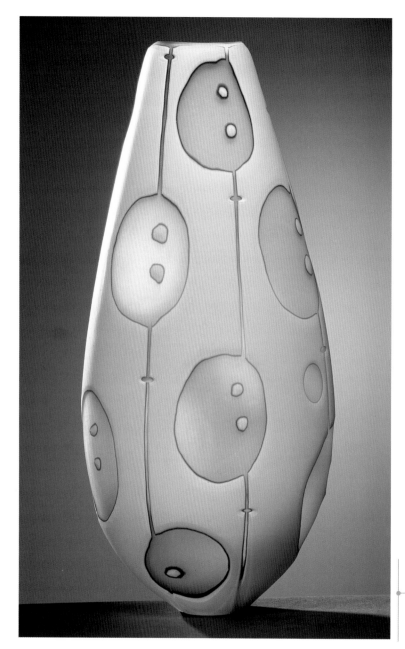

ETHAN STERN
Pickett, 2004

Blown glass; diamond and
stone-wheel engraved

Photo by John Lucas

JUDITH LA SCOLA
White Veiled Vessel, 2003

13 x 13 x 8 inches (33 x 33 x 20.3 cm)

Plate, blown, and cast glass, copper
base; sandblasted, painted, etched

Photo by Rob Vinnedge

DEBORA MOORE
Brassia Spider Orchid Leaf, 2002

16½ x 12 x 7 inches (41.9 x 30.5 x 17.8 cm)

Blown, sculpted glass

Photo by Lynn Thompson

These stones and vines have been witness. The ground is hallowed by those souls who have lived on it and loved on it, and who have been nurtured by it.

ELIZABETH RYLAND MEARS
Goblet with Grapevine: Harvest, 2003

10 x 6 x 6 inches (25.4 x 15.2 x 15.2 cm)
Flameworked glass
Photo by Tommy Elder

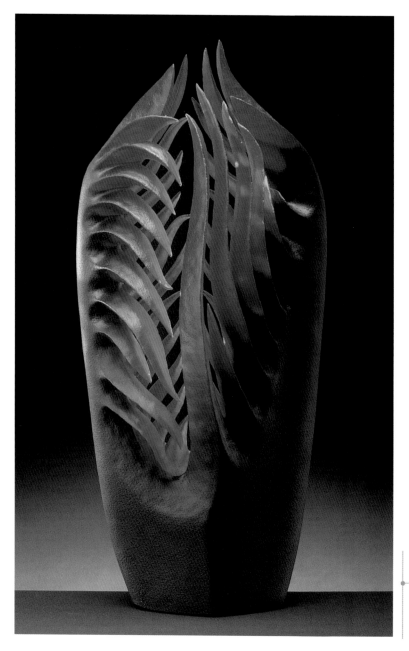

PAUL SCHWIEDER
Copper-Blue Prairie Wave, 2004

15 x 9 x 4 inches (38.1 x 22.9 x 10.2 cm)

Blown glass; sandblasted

Photo by Glenn Moody

Our work captures the movement of water, grasses, and other elements of the wetland surrounding our home and studio.

JAMES ENGEBRETSON
RENEE NIELSEN ENGEBRETSON
Leaf Vessel, 2003

10 x 7½ x 7½ inches
(25.4 x 19.1 x 19.1 cm)

Blown glass; multi-layered, sandblasted, carved

Photo by Don Pitlik

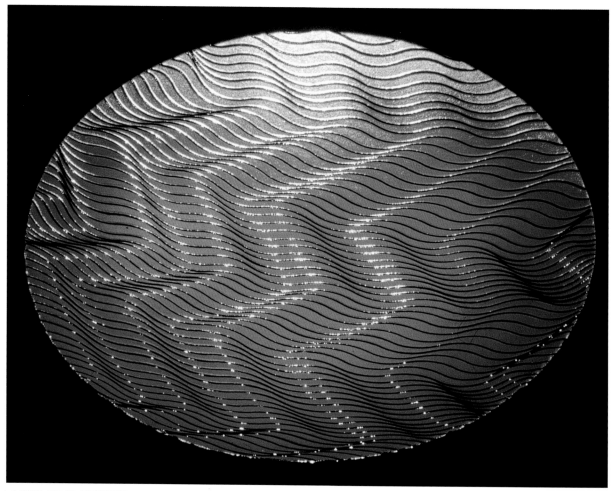

LINDA ELLIS ANDREWS
Ondulation: Les Illusions Series, 1999

15 x 15 x 2 inches (38.1 x 38.1 x 5 cm)

Fused and kiln-formed dichroic glass

Photo by artist

JOHN J. GECI
Peridot Green/Opal White Eclipse Bowl, 2004

5 x 13 x 7½ inches (12.7 x 33 x 19.1 cm)

Blown glass; incalmo, double-walled

Photo by Tom Mills

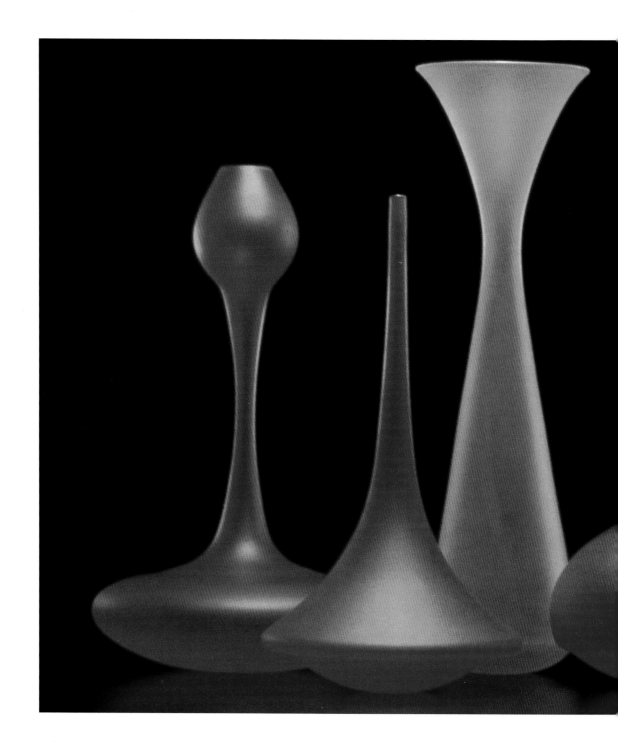

PABLO SOTO
Red & Orange Silhouettes, 2004

Tallest: 24 x 12 inches (61 x 30.5 cm)

Blown glass; acid etched

Photo by Tom Mills

ANTHONY SCHAFERMEYER
CLAIRE KELLY
Water Tower, 2002

20 x 6 inches (50.8 x 15.2 cm)

Blown glass; mosaic cane

Photo by H&O Photography

DICK MARQUIS
Elephant #03-1, 2003

10¾ x 5½ x 4½ inches
(27.3 x 14 x 11.4 cm)

Blown, hot-sculpted glass;
granulare technique

Photo by artist

123

I like to incorporate
other materials into
glass to express
harmony in nature.

MASAMI KODA
Link, 2002

24 x 9 x 9 inches (61 x 22.9 x 22.9 cm)

Lampworked glass, copper wire,
painted steel

Photo by artist

NAOKO TAKENOUCHI
Kataribe #13, 2004

13¾ x 9½ x 4 inches (35 x 24 x 10 cm)

Blown glass, silver foil, copper, natural fiber; multi-layered, sandblasted

Photo by Kenji Nagai

125

WARREN AND VAN HASSEL
Arches, 2005

8 x 9½ x 6 inches (20.3 x 24.1 x 15.2 cm)

Blown glass; drilled, carved, buffed,
acid washed

Photo by Fred Reincke

The "Butt Vase" series explores various stencil-oriented designs and airbrushed paint combinations. The rocking movement of these pieces contribute to their sense of whimsy and playfulness.

RICK MELBY
Polka Butt: Butt Vase Series, 2004

4 x 4 x 5½ inches (10.2 x 10.2 x 14 cm)

Blown glass; cut, ground, sandblasted, low-fire glass paint

Photos by Carl Powell

127

PABLO SOTO
Color Drops, 2004

16 x 14 inches (40.6 x 35.6 cm)

Blown glass; acid etched

Photo by Tom Mills

129

SHANE FERO
Blossom Bottle, 2003

25 x 8½ x 8½ inches (63.5 x 21.6 x 21.6 cm)

Hot-blown glass; flameworked,
sandblasted, acid etched; gaffed by John Geci

Photo by John Littleton

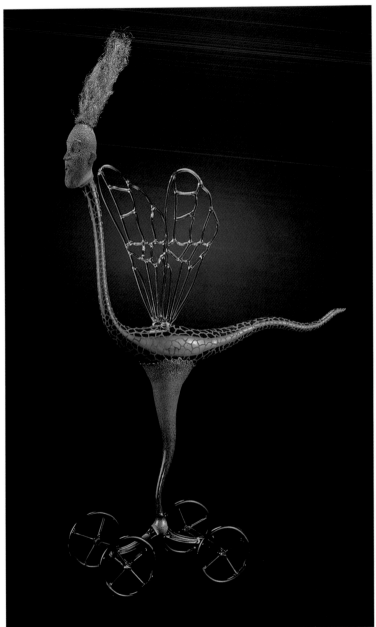

I look for the unexpected in my work and make a deliberate effort to cultivate surprises.

ROBERT MICKELSEN
Trekker, 2004

31 x 21 x 9 inches (78.7 x 53.3 x 22.9 cm)

Lampworked glass, steel wool; assembled, blown, sculpted

Photo by Dan Abbott

CHARLES PROVENZANO
Untitled, 2000

6 x 4 inches (15.2 x 10.2 cm)

Blown glass; zanferico and overlaid canes

Photo by Steven Berall

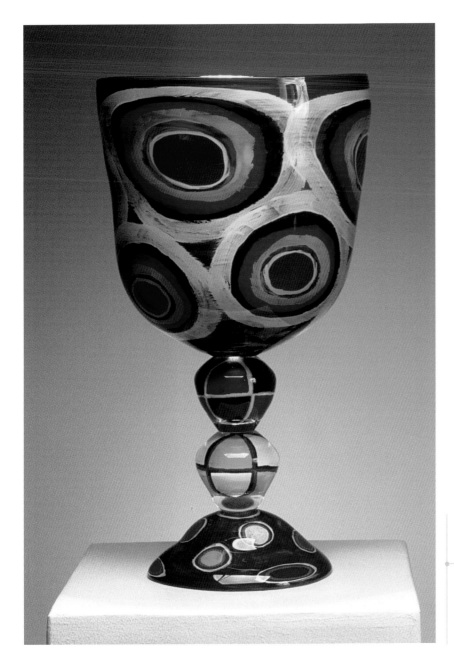

VALERIE BECK
RICK BECK
Footed Vessel, 2003

20 x 12 x 12 inches
(50.8 x 30.5 x 30.5 cm)

Blown glass; painted with enamels,
cased over

Photo by David Ramsey

KENNY PIEPER
Satellite Series, 2004

Left: 12 x 14 x 14 inches
(30.5 x 35.6 x 35.6 cm)
Right: 28 x 10 x 10 inches
(71.1 x 25.4 x 25.4 cm)

Blown glass; reticello and
primavera techniques

Photo by Jeff Mayer

DANIELLE BLADE
STEPHEN GARTNER
Strata-Covered Vessel with
Tied-Bone Finial, 2003

21 x 6 x 6 inches
(53.3 x 15.2 x 15.2 cm)

Blown, hot sculpted glass

Photo by Jonathan Wallen

WENDY HANNAM
Skyline (View) #1 & #2, 2003

Left: 15½ x 4¹⁵⁄₁₆ x 4¹⁵⁄₁₆ inches
(39.5 x 12.5 x 12.5 cm)
Right: 11 x 11 x 2¾ inches (28 x 28 x 7 cm)

Hand-blown glass; sandblasted, engraved

Photo by Grant Hancock

PABLO SOTO
Grey Silhouettes, 2004

Tallest: 30 x 8 inches (76.2 x 20.3 cm)

Blown glass; acid etched

Photo by Tom Mills

ETHAN STERN
Flame Target, 2004

Blown glass; diamond and
stone-wheel engraved

Photo by John Lucas

BENJAMIN SEWELL
Primordial, 2004

10⅝ x 11¹³⁄₁₆ x 4⁵⁄₁₆ inches (27 x 30 x 11 cm)

Hand-blown glass, red-hot glass inclusion;
diamond-wheel cut

Photo by Larry Irvin

SUSAN TAYLOR GLASGOW
Pinkies Out Coffee Cup, 2004

10 x 7 x 7 inches (25.4 x 17.8 x 17.8 cm)

Fused and sewn glass; slumped, sandblasted
photo imagery, glass enamel, waxed linen thread

Photos by artist

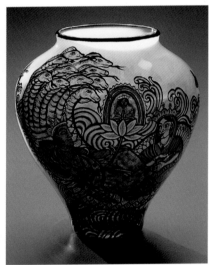

CAPPY THOMPSON
I Petition Lord Vishnu to Dream in His Cosmic Slumber of the Bodhisattva, 1996

15¾ x 14¼ x 14¼ inches (40 x 36.2 x 36.2 cm)

Blown glass, enamels; reverse painted

Photos by Michael Seidl

I like to celebrate the familiar, comforting objects that we all know and can relate to. Glass is a perfect medium to give these transient subjects permanence and importance.

TAMARA COATSWORTH
Jolly Time! 2004

8 x 3½ x 3½ inches (20.3 x 8.9 x 8.9 cm)

Fused glass, enamels; torchworked, sandblasted, acid etched

Photo by Gerry Slabaugh

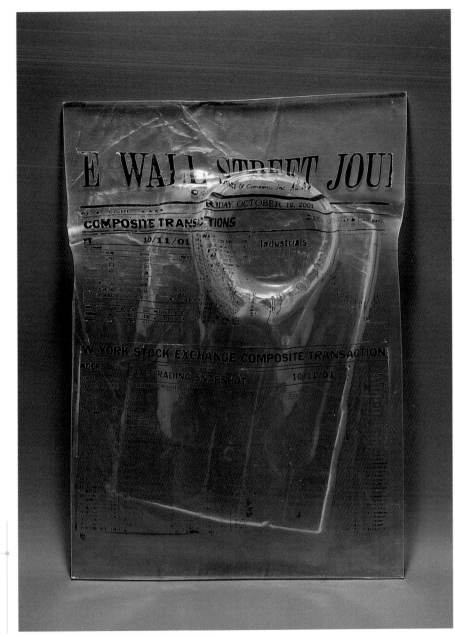

LAURA WARD
On the Surface, 2001

21 x 15 x 2½ inches
(53.3 x 38.1 x 6.4 cm)

Plate glass, photographic transfer;
enameled, sandblasted, kiln formed

Photo by Brian Heaton

KURT SWANSON
LISA SCHWARTZ
Jester Vase, 2004

15 x 7 x 5 inches (38.1 x 17.8 x 12.7 cm)

Blown glass

Photo by Bob Barrett

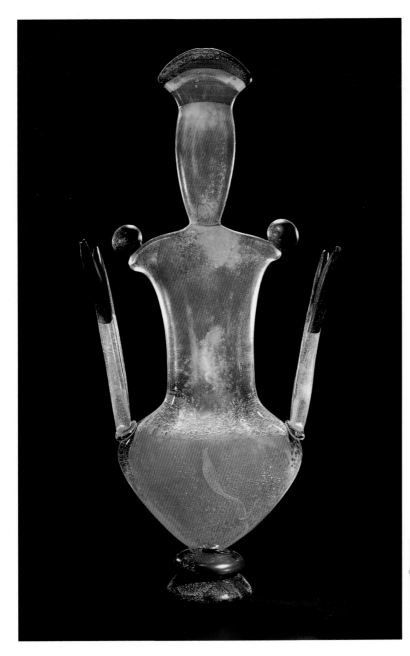

LOUIS SCLAFANI
Bottle Series, 1996

30 x 14 x 5 inches
(76.2 x 35.6 x 12.7 cm)

Hot-sculpted glass

Photo by Alex Casler

These sculptures are a reflection
of our ancestry and the many
stories yet to be uncovered.
They provoke our imaginations.

SABRINA KNOWLES
JENNY POHLMAN
Yggdrasil, Tree of Life, 2005

37 x 22 inches (94 x 55.9 cm)

Blown, sculpted glass, metal, beads

Photos by Russell Johnson

SABRINA KNOWLES
JENNY POHLMAN

ABOVE LEFT

Urd of the Norns, 2005

51 x 25 inches (129.5 x 63.5 cm)

Blown, sculpted glass, metal, beads

Photo by Russell Johnson

ABOVE RIGHT

Ancient One, 2005

36 x 26 x 16 inches (91.4 x 66 x 40.6 cm)

Blown, sculpted glass, metal, antique beads

Photo by Russell Johnson

JEINA MOROSOFF
Gathering/Grouping, 2000

Largest: 3 x 3 x 7 inches (7.6 x 7.6 x 17.8 cm)

Hand-blown glass; sandblasted

Photo by artist

This piece was created to explore glass as a transparent water metaphor. The overlapping transparency of the engraved image makes the depth seem limitless.

WENDY YOTHERS
Octopus Vase, 2004

6 x 8 x 4 inches
(15.2 x 20.3 x 10.2 cm)

Glass brick; engraved, hand polished, cold laminated

Photo by Dick Duane Studios

This is a kind of tribute
to one of my childhood
idols, "Big Daddy" Ed
Roth, who passed
away recently.

WES HUNTING
Hot Rod, 2004

32 x 18 x 14 inches (81.3 x 45.7 x 35.6 cm)

Hand-blown colored glass; sandblasted,
acid etched, assembled

Photo by Bill Lemke

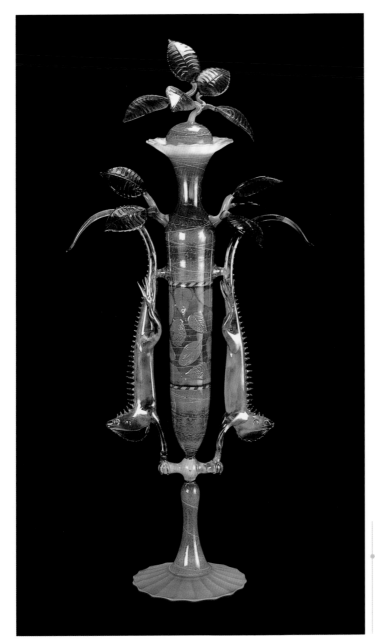

ROBERT MICKELSEN
Iguana Tree I, 2000

26½ x 12½ x 6 inches
(67.3 x 31.8 x 15.2 cm)

Blown, lampworked borosilicate glass;
graal technique, sculpted, sandblasted

Photo by artist

NANCY ARTHUR-McGEHEE
In the Garden, 2003

22½ x 6 inches (57.2 x 15.2 cm)

Production glass; sandblast
carved, engraved

Photos by artist

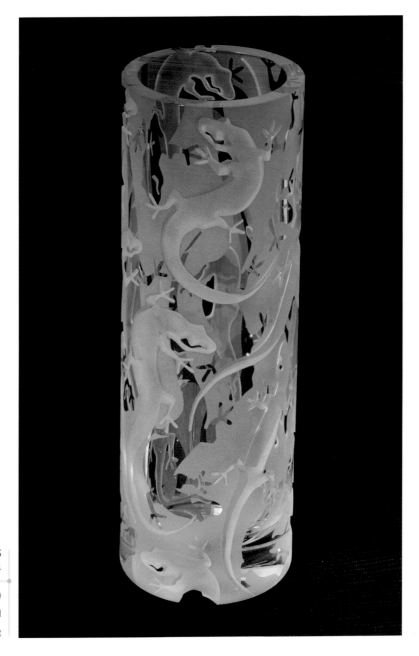

SYL MATHIS
Skinks, 2004

12 x 4 inches (30.5 x 10.2 cm)
Blown glass; deep-abrasive carved

Photo by artist

The inspiration for this piece stems from various textile designs and my love of pattern.

LISA SAMPHIRE
Lime Roll Up, 2004

14 x 9½ x 5½ inches (35.6 x 24.1 x 14 cm)

Blown incalmo with murrine; belted finish

Photos by Vince Klassen

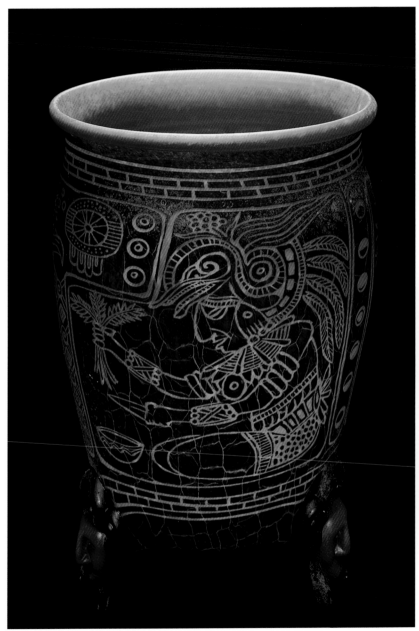

WILLIAM MORRIS
Engraved Urn, 2003

19 x 14 inches (48.3 x 35.6 cm)

Blown glass; engraved

Photos by Rob Vinnedge

SUSAN PLUM
Flor Amazonia, 2001

29 x 27 x 8 inches (73.7 x 68.6 x 20.3 cm)

Blown glass; flameworked, lacquered, spray enameled, cast

Photo by Lee Fatheree

CONCETTA MASON
It's OK, 2004

20 x 8½ x 8½ inches
(50.8 x 21.6 x 21.6 cm)

Blown glass; controlled breaking, sandblasted

Photo by Henry J. Ponter

157

LOUIS SCLAFANI
Bottle Series, 1996

31 x 13½ x 5 inches
(78.7 x 34.3 x 12.7 cm)

Hot-sculpted glass

Photo by Alex Casler

ANTHONY CORRADETTI
Spheres, 2004

20 x 14 x 14 inches
(50.8 x 35.6 x 35.6 cm)

Blown glass, opal white glass;
hand painted with glass lusters,
metal oxides, kiln fired

Photo by Sandra Rodger

CHARLES PROVENZANO
Goblet Set, 2000

7½ x 2½ inches each (19.1 x 6.4 cm)

Blown glass; transparent overlaid canes

Photo by Steven Berall

This piece is another in
the "Neo-Tassa" series.
The series is my interpretation
of classic Venetian
seventeenth-century forms.

dave myrick
Neo-Tassa #13, 2004

12 x 9 inches (30.5 x 22.9 cm)

Blown glass; multi-layered, engraved,
polished, assembled

Photo by Tom Mills

MARY VAN CLINE
The Floating Sea of Time, 2000

24 x 20 x 5 inches
(61 x 50.8 x 12.7 cm)

Photo-sensitive glass; pâte de verre

Photo by Rob Vinnedge

CHRISTOPHER McELROY
Coastal Range Teapot, 2004

9¼ x 4¾ x 4¾ inches (23.5 x 12.1 x 12.1 cm)

Borosilicate glass; flameworked, cold worked

Photo by artist

ANJA ISPHORDING
#60, 2001

13 x 6⅛ inches (33 x 16 cm)

Kiln-cast glass; lost-wax technique, cut, polished

Photo by Alfred Meibleham

FRITZ DREISBACH
*Midnight-Blue Waving
Mongo with Serpent, Ferns,
and Cast Base,* 1994

22½ x 23 x 13 inches
(57.2 x 58.4 x 33 cm)

Glass

Photo by artist

Making these miniature vessels is addictive. I love the fact that in a photo they look large, but are actually less than three inches tall. Jokingly, I refer to them as Barbie's Dreamhouse Collectibles.

MARYJANE MICHAUD
Day Lily, 2004

3 x ⅞ x 1¾ inches (7.6 x 2.2 x 4.5 cm)

Wound and blown borosilicate glass; multi-layered color, pulled sculpted petals, flameworked

Photo by Steve Gyurina

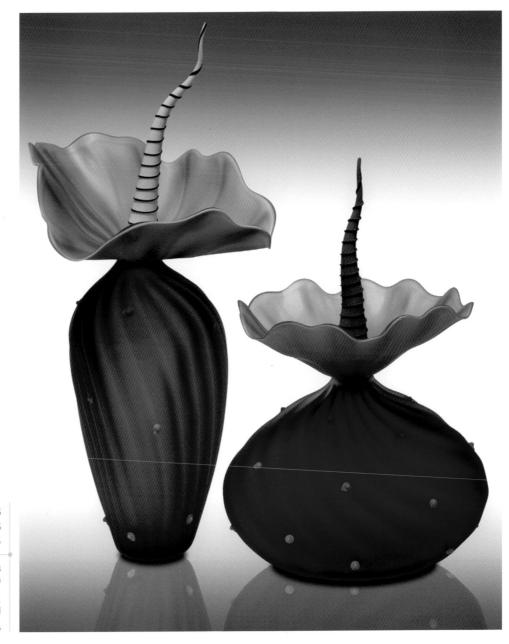

BOB KLISS
LAURIE KLISS
BOBtanical Grouping, 2005

Tallest: 16 x 7 x 7 inches
(40.6 x 17.8 x 17.8 cm)

Blown glass; joined hot,
sandblasted, acid etched

Photo by Laurie Montgomery

167

My work is narrative and often has elements of autobiography within a mythological content. In this vessel, the Noah story is represented, and my dog Canis and I are on board.

CAPPY THOMPSON
Safe Passage, 2000

27¼ x 15¾ x 15¾ inches (69.2 x 40 x 40 cm)
Blown glass, enamels; reverse-painted
Photos by Russell Johnson

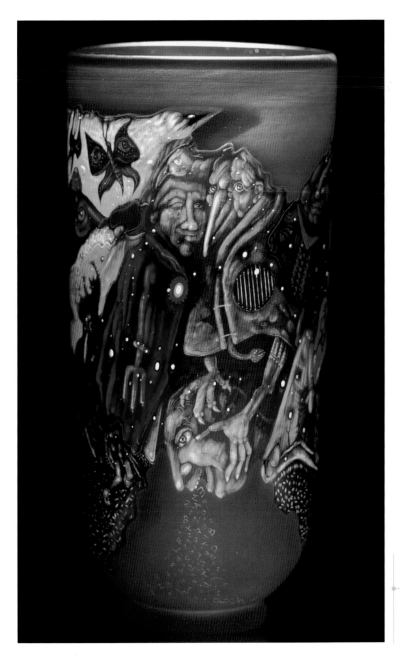

CHRISTIAN SCHMIDT
Words, 1999

11½ x 5½ x 5½ inches (29.5 x 14 x 14 cm)

Blown glass; multilayered, sandblasted, engraved

Photo by Lisa Moser

169

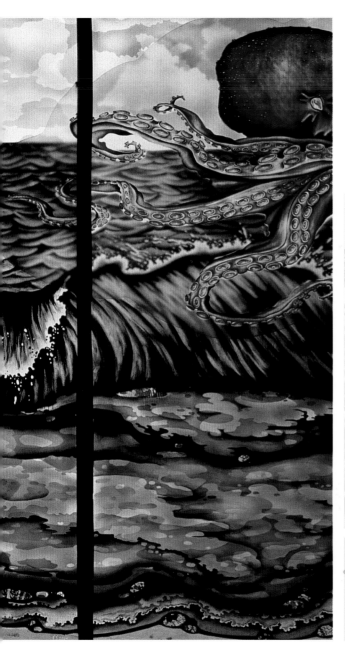

JUDITH SCHAECHTER
Dream of the Fisherman's Wife, 2004

32 x 48 inches (81.3 x 121.9 cm)

Stained glass, copper foil; sandblasted, engraved, enameled

Photos by Don Episcopo

171

CHRISTIAN SCHMIDT
Untitled, 2000

7⅔ x 7¼ inches (19.5 x 18.5 cm)

Blown glass; multi-layered,
sandblasted, engraved

Photo by A. Brandl
Detail photo by artist

VALERIE BECK
RICK BECK
Striped Cylinder, 2003

13 x 10 x 10 inches (33 x 25.4 x 25.4 cm)

Blown glass; painted with enamels, cased over

Photo by David Ramsey

JOHN J. GECI
Gold Eclipse Bowl, 2004

4½ x 12 x 5 inches (11.4 x 30.5 x 12.7 cm)

Blown glass; double-walled

Photo by Tom Mills

The Zen-like bowl form provides a peaceful home for the effervescence of champagne and the intrigue of distant constellations. The piece exudes a dynamic inner life that complements the simple, powerful form.

DAVID JAMES
Tranquiltity, Gold, 2000

4 x 20 inches (10.2 x 50.8 cm)
Kiln-cast lead crystal
Photo by André Cornellier

DANIELLE BLADE
STEPHEN GARTNER
*Batik-Covered Jar with Bone
and Tendril Finial,* 2004

17 x 7 x 7 inches (43.2 x 17.8 x 17.8 cm)

Blown glass; layered and manipulated
color, hot sculpted

Photo by Jonathan Wallen

SHANE FERO
Bamboo Bottles, 2004

Tallest: 13 x 2¾ x 2¾ inches
(33 x 7 x 7 cm)

Flameworked glass, gold leaf,
mother-of-pearl, gold loertz

Photo by John Littleton

177

STEVE BECKWITH
Blue Botanical, 2003

13 x 8 x 5 inches (33 x 20.3 x 12.7 cm)

Blown glass; sculpted, hot and cold
applications, sandblasted

Photo by Randall Smith

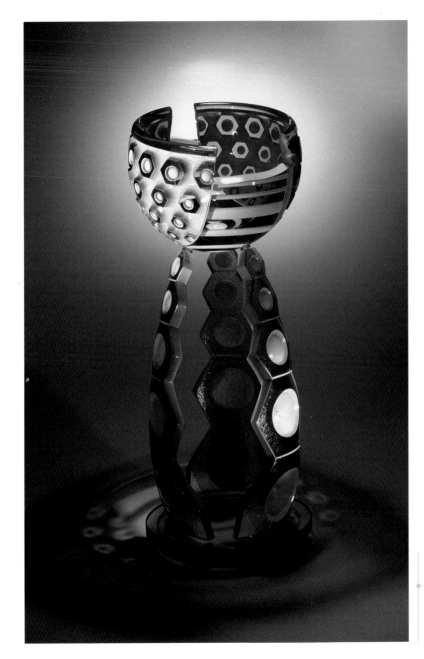

CONCETTA MASON
Sky of Blue, 2004

20 x 8 x 8 inches (50.8 x 20.3 x 20.3 cm)

Blown glass; controlled breaking, sandblasted

Photo by Henry J. Ponter

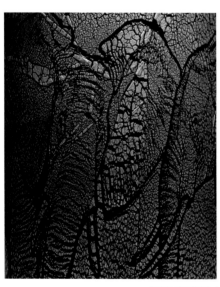

LISA CERNY
Ele-Fancy, 2003

16 x 5 x 5 inches (40.6 x 12.7 x 12.7 cm)

Blown glass; graal technique with
silver foil, etched, cold assembled

Photos by artist

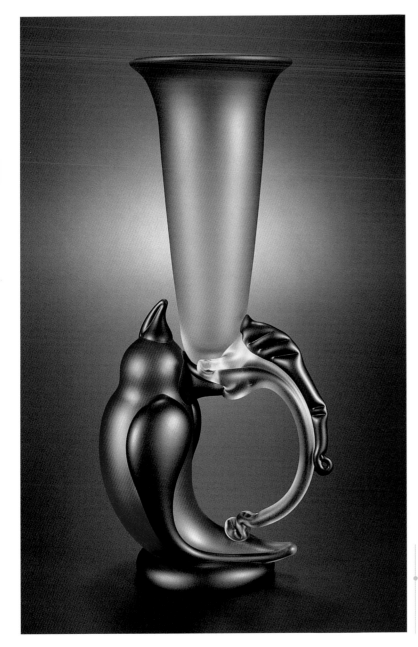

ROBERT LEVIN
Bird Goblet, 2003

13 x 6 x 3½ inches (33 x 15.2 x 8.9 cm)

Blown glass; frosted, sandblasted, acid etched

Photo by artist

181

MORNA TUDOR
Heart and Soul (#70-15), 2004

7 x 9½ x 9½ inches (17.8 x 24.1 x 24.1 cm)

Blown glass; reverse-painted, cut, polished

Photo by Vince Klassen

WENDY HANNAM
Greyscape, 2003

10⁷⁄₁₆ x 10⁷⁄₁₆ x 3⅛ inches
(26.5 x 26.5 x 8 cm)

Hand-blown glass; color
overlay, sandblasted, engraved

Photo by Grant Hancock

It's intriguing how the dichroic coatings will reflect and transmit different colors at the same time. The object will also refract lights and color of its environment.

ROBERT W. STEPHAN
His Light is Purer, 2004

5¾ x 5¾ x 5¾ inches
(14.6 x 14.6 x 14.6 cm)

Lead crystal, optical crystal, dichroic-optical inclusions; cut, laminated, ground, polished

Photos by Mark Bolick

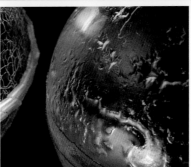

CAROLE FRÈVE
Quiet Moment, 2004

8 x 10 x 10 inches each (20.3 x 25.4 x 25.4 cm)

Blown, kiln-cast glass, electroplated copper, knitted-copper wire, glass beads

Photos by Michel Dubreuil

SUSAN TAYLOR GLASGOW
Act-Like-A-Lady Toaster Cozy, 2004

15½ x 11 x 5½ inches (39.4 x 27.9 x 14 cm)

Fused and sewn glass; slumped, sandblasted photo imagery, glass enamel, waxed linen thread, buttons

Photos by artist

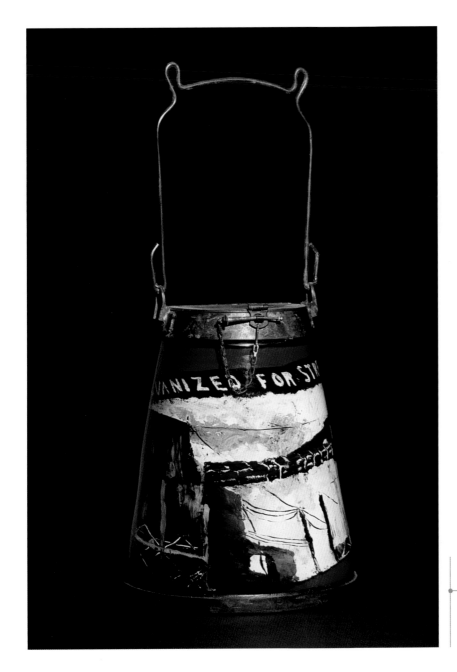

MAGAN STEVENS
Oilcan Series, 2000

22 x 15 x 15 inches (55.9 x 38.1 x 38.1 cm)

Blown glass, mixed media; reverse-painted

Photo by Pat Simone

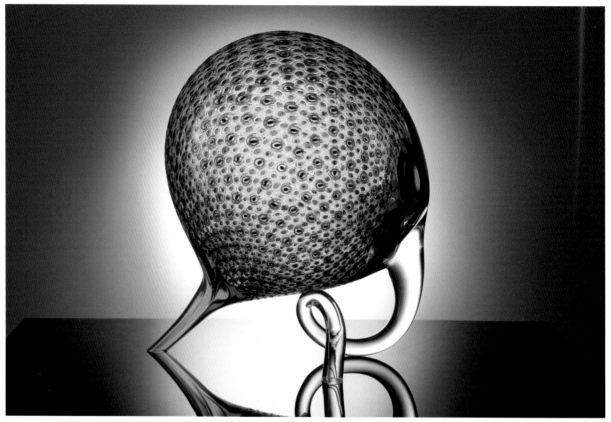

STEPHEN ROLFE POWELL
Lascivious Nubile Nudge, 2004

25 x 23 x 18½ inches (63.5 x 58.4 x 47 cm)

Blown glass; murrini surface

Assisted by Chris Bohach, Jon Capps, Matt
Cummings, Paul Hugues, Ted Jeckering

Photos by David Harpe

LAURA DONEFER
Tofino Amulet Basket, 2004

19 x 24 x 16 inches (48.3 x 61 x 40.6 cm)

Blown glass, turquoise, malachite;
torch worked

Photos by Steven Wild

After visiting the tidal pools of Tofino, British Columbia, Canada. I made this piece, thinking of purple and orange sea stars, green anemone, and waves, and how much I miss the sea.

189

The Element Series depicts a large, complex dialogue that begins with an "object" or a "verb." The finished piece, though complex, is built from smaller, simple elements.

BRENT KEE YOUNG
Sit: Element Series, 2003

42 x 18 x 20 inches (106.7 x 45.7 x 50.8 cm)
Heat-resistant glass; flameworked
Assisted by Yoshiko Asai.
Photo by Dan Fox/Lumina

In this eternal-flame memory piece, the eggs represent what is left behind after loss—values, memories—ready to hatch long after the loss has been felt.

TIM TATE

ABOVE LEFT
Fragile, 2004

14 x 10 x 5 inches (35.6 x 25.4 x 12.7 cm)
Blown glass, egg shells
Photo by Pete Duvall

ABOVE RIGHT
Gossamer, 2004

14 x 10 x 5 inches (35.6 x 25.4 x 12.7 cm)
Blown glass, feathers
Photo by Pete Duvall

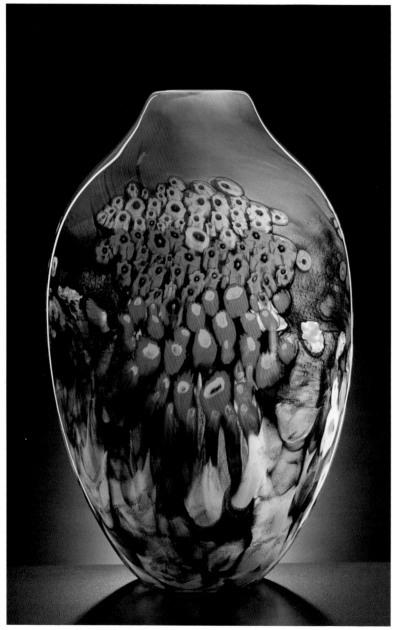

I have tried to incorporate my fondness for flowers and gardens with glass to create an impressionistic vision of the landscape. For me, flowers are small worlds, filled with colors and shapes that produce incredible beauty. My intention is to evoke a feeling of serenity and solitude—a homage to nature.

SHAWN E. MESSENGER
Landscape Series Vase, 2004

11 x 7 x 7 inches (27.9 x 17.8 x 17.8 cm)

Blown glass; multi-layered

Photo by Tommy Olof Elder

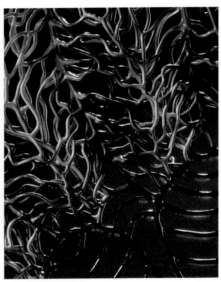

SUSAN PLUM
Mandragora (Mandrake), 2001

34 x 26 x 8 inches (86.4 x 66 x 20.3 cm)

Blown glass; cast, flameworked, lacquered, enameled

Photos by Lee Fatheree

KENNY PIEPER
Clay, 2004

13 x 14 x 14 inches (33 x 35.6 x 35.6 cm)

Blown glass; reticello, incalmo, solid
sculpting, sandblasted, acid etched

Photo by Tom Mills

WILLIAM BERNSTEIN
Figure Goblet, 1995

14½ x 5 x 5 inches (36.8 x 12.7 x 12.7 cm)

Blown, hot-tooled glass

Photo by J. Littleton

CHRISTIAN SCHMIDT
In Orange um halb vier, 2002

8⅔ x 7⅞ x 7⅞ inches
(22 x 20 x 20 cm)

Blown glass; multi-layered,
engraved

Photo by Lisa Moser

HANS GODO FRÄBEL
*Hanging Around: Clown
Series No. 64,* 2003

14½ inches high (36.8 cm)

Lampworked, clear blown
glass; sandblasted
Vase created by Paul Bendzunas

Photo by Yasuko Rudisill

KATE VOGEL
JOHN LITTLETON
Topsy Turvy, 2004

14 x 8 x 6⅛ inches (35.6 x 20.3 x 15.6 cm)

Cast, hot-formed, faceted glass,
gold leaf, mica, fiberglass

Photos by artist

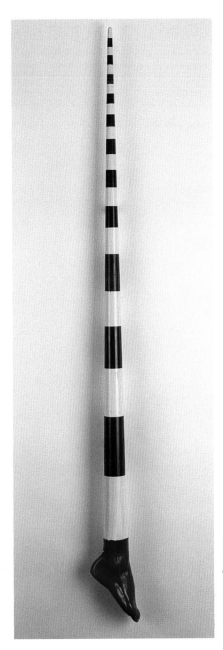

This work is based on the statement "Run with the heart of the blind."

BRENT COLE
Blindspot, 2002

78 x 6 x 5 inches
(198.1 x 15.2 x 12.7 cm)

Mold-blown glass, mixed media

Photo by artist

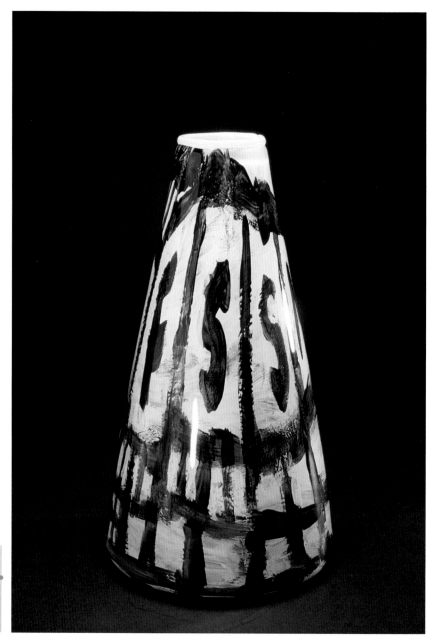

JOHN DRURY
Untitled, 1998

16 x 9 x 9 inches (40.6 x 22.9 x 22.9 cm)

Blown glass

Photo by artist

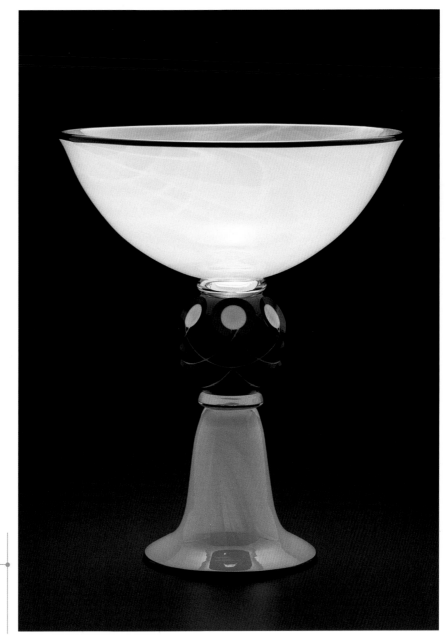

dave myrick
Neo-Tassa #14, 2004

11 x 10 inches (27.9 x 25.4 cm)

Blown glass; multi-layered,
engraved, polished, assembled

Photo by Tom Mills

I find glass an excellent medium for
exploring life's vulnerabilities.

BANDHU SCOTT DUNHAM
Multicolored Basket, 2005

7 x 12 x 12 inches (17.8 x 30.5 x 30.5 cm)
Borosilicate glass; lampworked, sandblasted
Photo by artist

ETHAN STERN
Meiosis, 2004

Blown glass; diamond and
stone-wheel engraved

Photos by John Lucas

JULIA REIMER
Mackintosh Vases, 2004

Tallest: 17 x 4½ x 4½ inches
(43.2 x 11.4 x 11.4 cm)

Blown glass

Photo by John Dean

From milk bottles to enameled juice glasses, my work draws from a common pool of '50s pop nostalgia. In creating work that is similar to that of machine-made objects, I challenge the viewer to distinguish the two, further testing the notion of truth and pre-fabricated memory.

JULIE GIBB
best before, 2003

10¼ x 9¹³⁄₁₆ x 4⅓ inches each
(26 x 25 x 11 cm)

Blown glass; enameled

Photo by artist

GINNY RUFFNER
The Legend of the Banana Split, 2005

22 x 17 x 4 inches (55.9 x 43.2 x 10.2 cm)

Glass, mixed media

Photo by Mike Seidl

PAUL J. STANKARD
Cloistered Assemblage, 2002

8 x 7 x 5 inches (20.3 x 17.8 x 12.7 cm)

Glass; cold worked, flameworked

Photo by John Healey

DAVID SVENSON
Running Marathon, 1994

26 x 48 x 14 inches each
(66 x 121.9 x 35.6 cm)

Glass tubing, neon

Photo by Robert Taylor

Ecstasy in Spring celebrates the arrival of the season and all the potential of the coming year.

MARK VANDENBERG
Ecstasy in Spring, 2003

17 x 6 x 6 inches (43.2 x 15.2 x 15.2 cm)
Blown, lampworked glass
Photo by Leslie Patron

ADRIENNE McSTAY
Dancing Goblets, 1989

12 x 4 x 4 inches each
(30.5 x 10.2 x 10.2 cm)

Blown glass

Photo by artist

BRIAN F. RUSSELL
Hemisphere 112 Tempest, 2004

15 x 25 x 15 inches
(38.1 x 63.5 x 38.1 cm)

Cast glass, forged steel

Photo by artist

FLO PERKINS
Nova, 2004

51 x 48 x 55 inches
(129.5 x 121.9 x 139.7 cm)

Blown glass, steel, bronze

Photo by Addison Doty

JESSE J. RASID
Green Scirocco Tuxedo (Vase), 2002

18 x 7 x 7 inches (45.7 x 17.8 x 17.8 cm)
Blown glass
Photo by artist

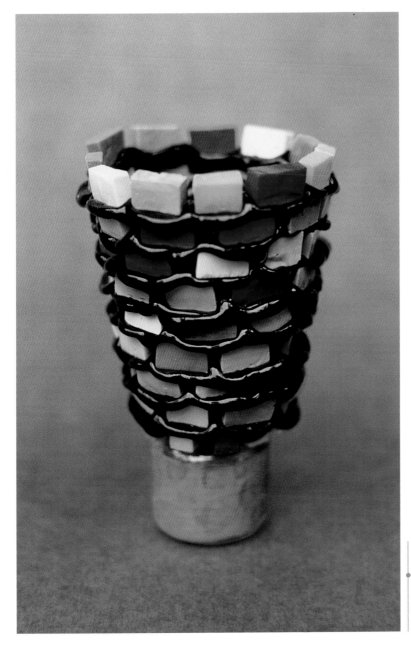

JOHN DRURY
Untitled, 2001

7 x 4 x 4 inches (17.8 x 10.2 x 10.2 cm)

Glass, rubber

Photo by artist

CARLOS LUIS ZERVIGÓN
Monster Glass, 2004

5½ x 3 x 3 inches each (14 x 7.6 x 7.6 cm)

Blown glass, copper wire;
multi-layered, crackled

Photo by artist

BENJAMIN W. COBB
Vessel Containers, 2001

18 x 8 x 8 inches each
(45.7 x 20.3 x 20.3 cm)

Blown glass, rubber; cut, assembled

Photos by Hector Sanchez

The colors in nature interest
me; in particular the colors
of butterflies, especially when
they are seen up close,
as under a microscope.
I am inspired by things that
intrinsically spiral, such as
whirlpools or tops launched
from the hand.

KATHLEEN MULCAHY
Fire and Ice, 2000

18 x 18 x 19 inches
(45.7 x 45.7 x 48.3 cm)

Blown glass

Photo by artist

JASON MORRISSEY
Set of Glass Spheres, 2004

2 x 1¾ inches each (5.1 x 4.5 cm)

Borosilicate glass; silver-
and gold-fumed implosion

Photos by Robert Diamante

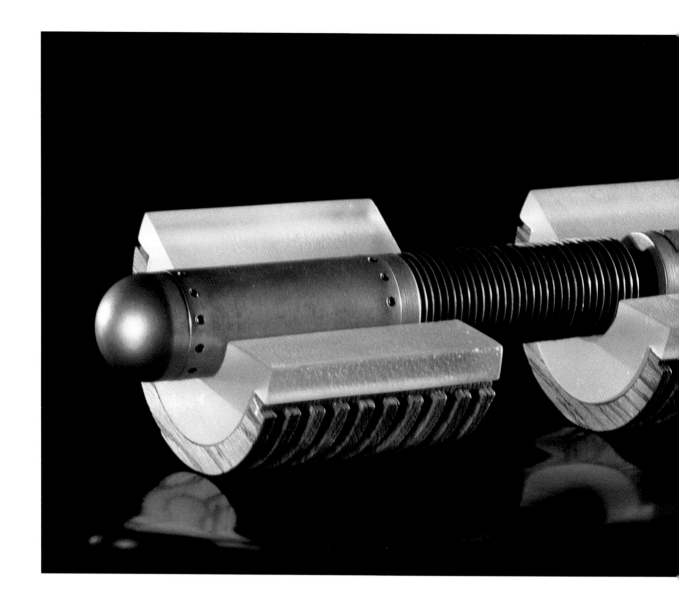

M. SEAN MERCER
LGT-MQ-1-3, 2004

5 x 5 x 23 inches (12.7 x 12.7 x 58.4 cm)

Glass, wood, steel, brass

Photo by Eva Heyd

I am interested in the relationship of overlapping patterns and multiple-container forms.

KEN CARDER
LEFT

Serpentine Progression Series, 2005

19 x 8½ x 4½ inches (48.3 x 21.6 x 11.4 cm)

Mold-blown glass, copper, bronze, silver, fabricated metal

Photo by artistmetal

ABOVE

Serpentine Progression Series, 2005

23 x 9 x 4½ inches (58.4 x 22.9 x 11.4 cm)

Mold-blown glass, copper, bronze, silver, fabricated metal

Photo by artist

My commitment to strong, classical, three-dimensional form is integral to my concept and approach. It is the linchpin of my oeuvre; it is the canvas on which I paint.

JOEL PHILIP MYERS
Canvas #14, 2004

14 x 7 x 7 inches (35.6 x 17.8 x 17.8 cm)

Mold-blown glass; sharded, partially enameled

Photo by John Herr

223

FREDERICK BIRKHILL
Curio Cabinet, 1993

17 x 10 x 10 inches
(43.2 x 25.4 x 25.4 cm)

Flameworked glass, mixed media,
wood, paint

Photo by artist

LUCY LYON
Public Library, 2003

21 x 20 x 19 inches
(53.3 x 50.8 x 48.3 cm)

Cast-glass figures, fabricated
aluminum, stained glass

Photo by Addison Doty

DAVID SVENSON
*Ken & Barbie Visit the
Floating World,* 1999

16 x 16 x 16 inches
(40.6 x 40.6 x 40.6 cm)

Mold-blown, phosphor-coated
glass, neon, mixed media

Photo by Robert Taylor

LUCY LYON
Last Table, 2002

14 x 26 x 17 inches (35.6 x 66 x 43.2 cm)

Cast-glass figures, fabricated steel,
fused glass

Photo by Addison Doty

227

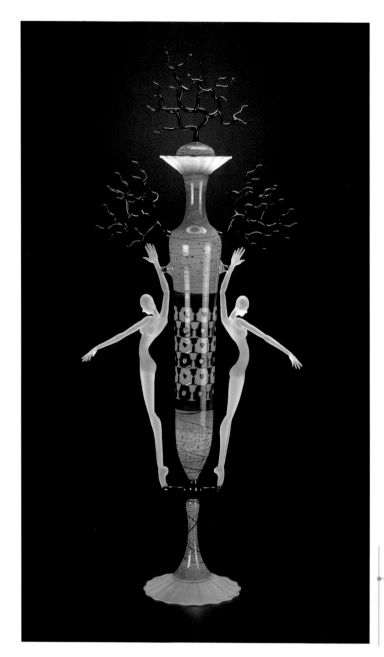

ROBERT MICKELSEN
Truth Has Two Faces, 2001

30½ x 13 x 6 inches (77.5 x 33 x 15.2 cm)

Blown, lampworked borosilicate glass; graal technique, sculpted, sandblasted

Photo by artist

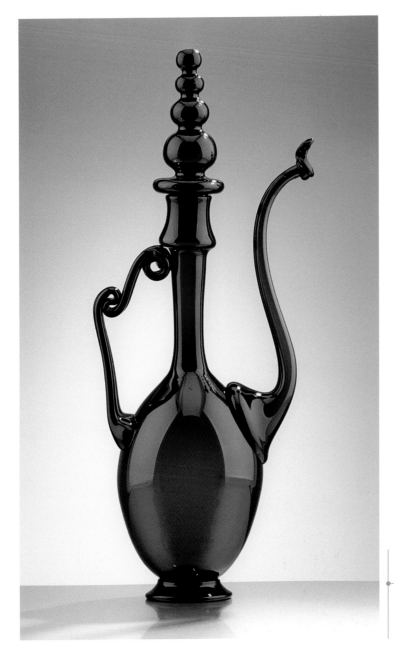

JEFF MACK
Amethyst Spouted Ewer, 2004

12 x 6 x 3½ inches (30.5 x 15.2 x 8.9 cm)

Blown glass

Photo by Leslie Patron

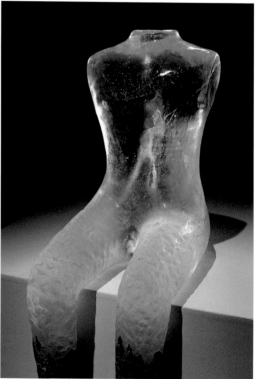

CAROLE PILON
Les Corps Étrangers II, 2004

40¹⁵⁄₁₆ x 10¼ x 6¾ inches (104 x 26 x 17 cm)

Lost-wax cast crystal, paper pulp, pigments

Photos by Michel Dubreuil

KATE VOGEL
JOHN LITTLETON
Tree of Life, 1997–1998

Top: 15¼ x 13½ inches (38.7 x 34.3 cm)
Base: 13¾ inches (34.9 cm)

Blown and cast glass; electroplated
base with copper

Photo by artist

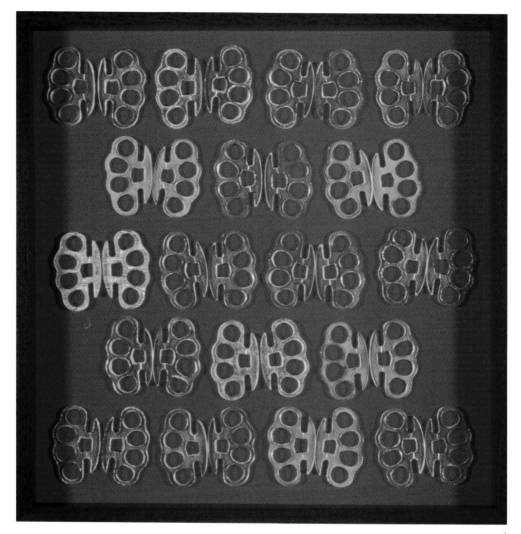

JACQUELINE KNIGHT
Night Patrol: Knuckle Dusters, 2002

23⅝ x 23⅝ x 2¾ inches (60 x 60 x 7 cm)

Cast lead crystal, stainless steel, matting board, frame; engraved

Photo by A.N.U. Photography

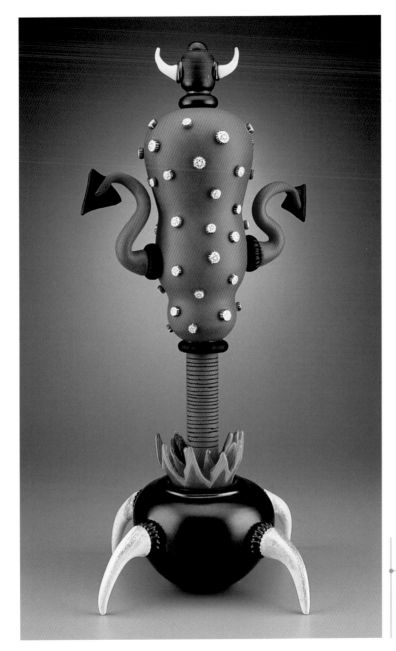

WES HUNTING
Satan's Parfume, 2004

34 x 13 x 16 inches (86.4 x 33 x 40.6 cm)

Hand-blown colored glass; sandblasted, acid etched, assembled

Photo by Bill Lemke

Created in collaboration with my daughter, L. Lindsey Mears, who is a book artist, poet, and photographer.

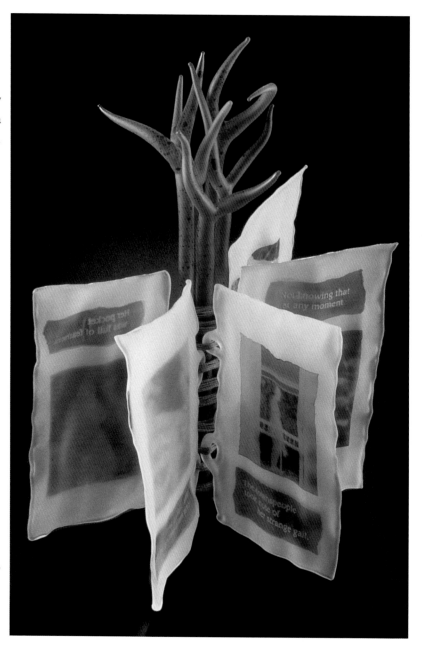

ELIZABETH RYLAND MEARS
Standing Book: Pocket Full of Feathers, 2004

13 x 10 x 7 inches (33 x 25.4 x 17.8 cm)

Glass, lusters, photo images, waxed linen; flameworked, sandblasted

Photo by Tommy Elder

This piece focuses on the sinister aspects of life—frightening yet beautiful

FREDERICK BIRKHILL
In the Arbor of Good and Evil, 2004

17 x 13 x 3½ inches (43.2 x 33 x 8.9 cm)

Flameworked glass, wood, paint; enameled;

Photo by artist

235

PHILIPPA BEVERIDGE
The Inevitability of Loss, 2003–2004

41⅓ x 21½ x 1⅕ inches
(105 x 55 x 3 cm) each panel

Cast glass, textiles, steel; cold worked,
printed, lost-wax method

Photo by artist

KAREN KOROBOW-MAIN
Untitled #26, 2004

7 x 13 x 2 inches each (17.8 x 33 x 5 cm)

Cast-glass bas relief, oil paints

Photo by Mel Schockner

JAMES ENGEBRETSON
RENEE NIELSEN ENGEBRETSON
Flaming Glass Vessel, 2003

14½ x 11 x 10½ inches
(36.8 x 27.9 x 26.7 cm)

Blown glass; multi-layered, sandblasted

Photo by Don Pitlik

STEVEN E. MAIN
Fire Series Sculpted Vase, 2004

7½ x 6 x 3 inches (19 x 15.2 x 7.6 cm)

Hand-blown glass; color stacked, cane pickup, sandblasted, cut, polished

Photo by Mel Schockner

239

TAKAYA TOKIZAWA
Moonlit Vases, 2005

Tallest: 12½ x 3⅜ inches (31.8 x 8.6 cm)

Blown glass, silver leaf

Photo by Russell Johnson

STEVE KLEIN
Balance IV, 2004

18 x 12 x 2½ inches
(45.7 x 30.5 x 6.4 cm)

Kiln-formed, blown glass

Photo by Jason Van Fleet

JUDITH LA SCOLA
Turquoise Ripple

18 x 13 x 9 inches (45.7 x 33 x 22.9 cm)

Plate and blown glass, copper base;
sandblasted, painted, etched

Photos by Rob Vinnedge

PENELOPE WURR
Pajama-Stripe Bud Vases, 1998

10 x 2¼ x 2¼ inches
(25.4 x 5.7 x 5.7 cm)

Mold-blown glass; my patented
translucent-enamel overlay

Photo by artist

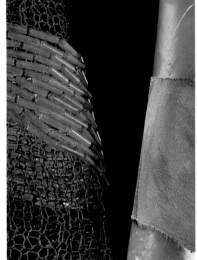

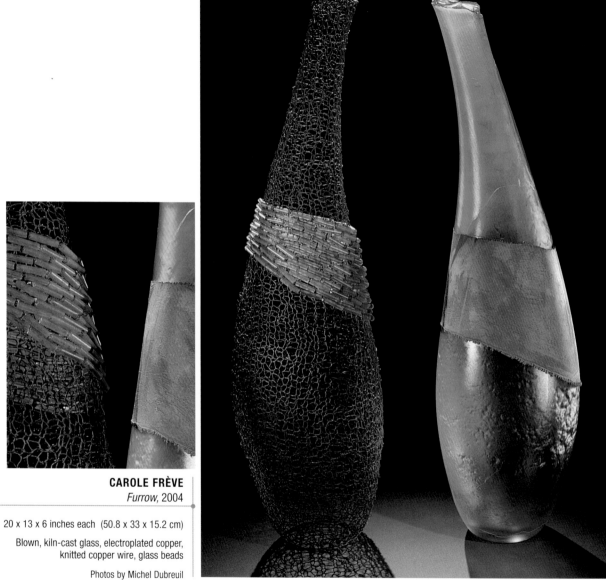

CAROLE FRÈVE
Furrow, 2004

20 x 13 x 6 inches each (50.8 x 33 x 15.2 cm)

Blown, kiln-cast glass, electroplated copper,
knitted copper wire, glass beads

Photos by Michel Dubreuil

CAROLE FRÈVE
Storm Series: Frimas, 2004

15 x 13 x 6 inches each (38.1 x 33 x 15.2 cm)

Blown, kiln-cast glass, electroplated copper, knitted copper wire, glass beads

Photos by Michel Dubreuil

245

KATRINA HUDE
Red Zinger Barbells, 2002

3 x 10 x 3 inches each
(7.6 x 25.4 x 7.6 cm)

Blown glass, murrini; wheel carved,
acid etched

Photo by artist

KATRINA HUDE
ABOVE LEFT

Hope Barbells, 2004

3 x 8 x 3 inches each (7.6 x 20.3 x 7.6 cm)

Blown glass, murrini; wheel carved,
acid etched

Photo by artist

LEFT
Blue Heart Barbells, 2003

3 x 10 x 3 inches each (7.6 x 25.4 x 7.6 cm)

Blown glass, murrini; wheel carved,
acid etched

Photo by artist

This work is a family portrait.
The structure of family, couples,
and siblings—being part and apart—
determines placement and
consequent dialogue.

DEBORAH HORRELL
Still Life: Purity of a Dream, 2003

14½ x 19½ x 11½ inches
(36.8 x 49.5 x 29.2 cm)

Cast glass; pâte de verre, solid cast

Photo by Paul Foster

STEPHAN COX
Orange Bud with Gold Spikes, 2004

12 x 8 x 8 inches (30.5 x 20.3 x 20.3 cm)

Hand-blown glass; segmented,
carved, cold fused

Photo by Don Pitlik

KATE VOGEL
JOHN LITTLETON
Portal, 2003

16 x 7¾ x 4½ inches (40.6 x 19.7 x 11.4 cm)

Cast glass, hot formed and cast
mica, fiberglass, gold leaf

Photo by artist

JEINA MOROSOFF
Standing Tenticles, 2004

16 x 3 x 3 inches
(40.6 x 7.6 x 7.6 cm)

Blown glass; sandblasted

Photo by Femke Van Delft

JUDITH SHAPIRO
Solar Shift, 2004

19 x 19 x 1½ inches (48.3 x 48.3 x 3.8 cm)

Multi-layered glass; fused, slumped, sandblasted, cold worked

Photo by Jonathan Wallen

LAURA DONEFER
Gaia Amulet Basket, 2005

18 x 20 x 11 inches (45.7 x 50.8 x 27.9 cm)

Blown glass, shards, turquoise, wool, eggshell beads, coral; torch worked

Photo by Steven Wild

JAMES MONGRAIN
Modern Venetians, Cobalt, 2004

Tallest: 10 x 2¾ inches (25.4 x 7 cm)

Blown glass

Photo by Russell Johnson

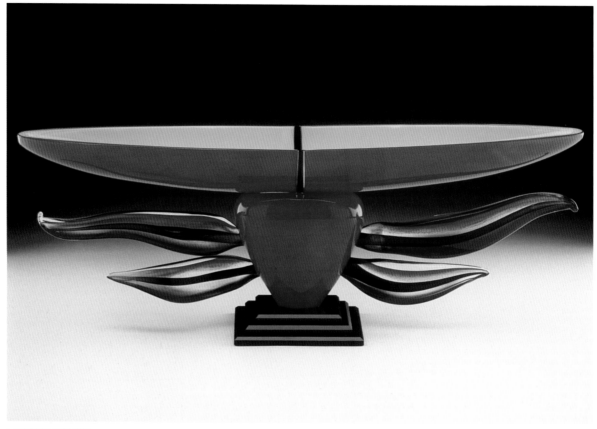

RANDY STRONG
Winged Bowl, 2004

9 x 26½ x 6 inches (22.9 x 67.3 x 15.2 cm)

Blown glass; cold fused
Photo by Keay Edwards

KURT SWANSON
LISA SCHWARTZ
Pinkichinno Goblets, 2004

Average height: 9 inches (22.9 cm)

Hand-blown glass

Photo by Bob Barrett

Using a combination of sandblasting and translucent-enamel overlay, I created a graphic finish more reminiscent of textiles than of glass.

PENELOPE WURR
Tall Squiggly Vase, 2000

12 x 5¾ x 5¾ inches
(30.5 x 14.6 x 14.6 cm)

Mold-blown glass; translucent
enamel overlay

Photo by artist

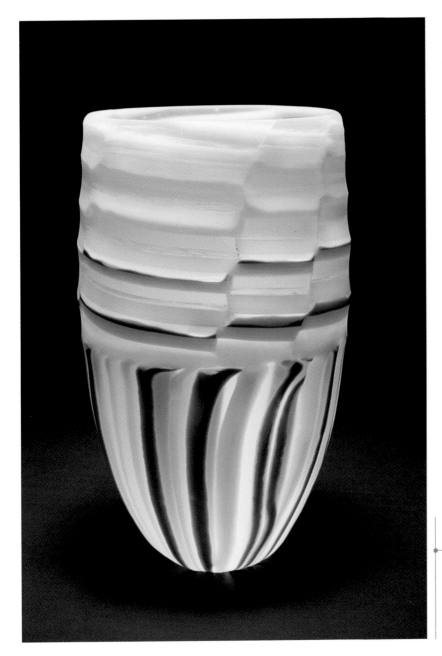

JOHNATHON SCHMUCK
Unconformity #36, 2000

11 x 6 x 6 inches (27.9 x 15.2 x 15.2 cm)

Incalmo-blown, fused glass; roll up,
wheel cut, belt sanded, acid etched

Co-produced with Ruth Allen in New Zealand

Photo by Haru Sameshima

STEVE KLEIN
Balance VI, 2004

5 x 21 x 21 inches
(12.7 x 53.3 x 53.3 cm)

Kiln-formed, blown glass

Photo by Jason Van Fleet

JASON MORRISSEY
Two-Sided Glass Sphere, 2004

2 inches diameter (5.1 cm)

Blown borosilicate glass; 24-karat-gold fumed

Photos by Robert Diamante

261

In the dark heat of the kiln, shapes open and close, twist about, or become tense and then relax. The final sculpture freezes a moment that is both stable and dynamic.

JANET KELMAN
Sunset Seafan, 2004

9½ x 21 x 19 inches (24.1 x 53.3 x 48.3 cm)
Blown glass; sandblasted, slumped
Photo by Leslie Patron

The sunrays are clear protrusions, formed when the last gather of clear glass is taken. They act like prisms, playing with light and reflecting all the colors and shapes around them.

SOL MAYA
Fragile Balance, 2004

Top: 16 x 18 x 2½ inches
(40.6 x 45.7 x 6.4 cm)
Bottom: series, 22 x 24 x 4 inches
(55.9 x 61 x 10.2 cm)

Hand-blown glass

Photo by Gwen Poole

DAVID SCHNUCKEL
Commemorating Heroes at Their Worst, 2003

Tallest: 27 inches (68.6 cm)

Blown glass, ink, enamel

Photo by Don Distell

KATHERINE BERNSTEIN
WILLIAM BERNSTEIN
Face Pitcher, 2002

5½ x 4½ x 3½ inches
(14 x 11.4 x 8.9 cm)

Blown glass; hot cane drawing

Photo by J. Littleton

The idea behind this piece is that we are the weavers of our life tapestry, assisted by the radiant divine energy of the universe. I am the dream weaver, and the tapestry I am weaving is the image that wraps the vessel—of my husband Charlie and me as lovers/deities.

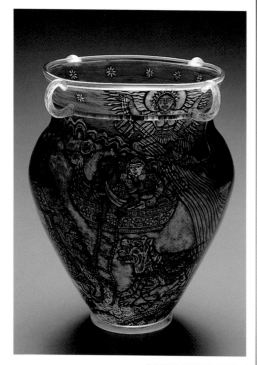

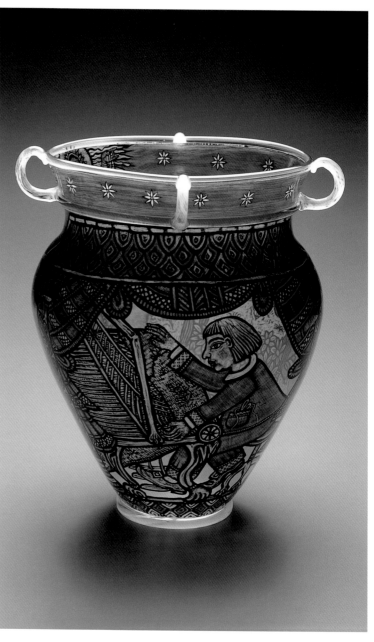

CAPPY THOMPSON
Dream Tapestry, 1999

15¾ x 13½ x 13½ inches
(40 x 34.3 x 34.3 cm)

Blown glass, enamels;
reverse painted

Photos by Michael Seidl

DAN DAILEY
Fox Man, 1997

15½ x 12 x 12 inches
(39.4 x 30.5 x 30.5 cm)

Hand-blown glass, enamel;
sandblasted, acid polished

Photo by Bill Truslow

267

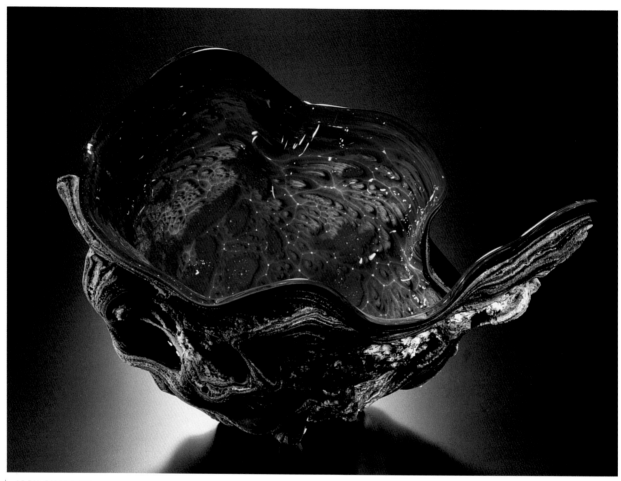

JOSH SIMPSON
Blue New Mexico Tektite, 2004

11 x 16 x 14½ inches (27.9 x 40.6 x 36.8 cm)

Blown glass, meteorite glass sculpture;
reactive silver decoration

Photo by Tommy Olof Elder

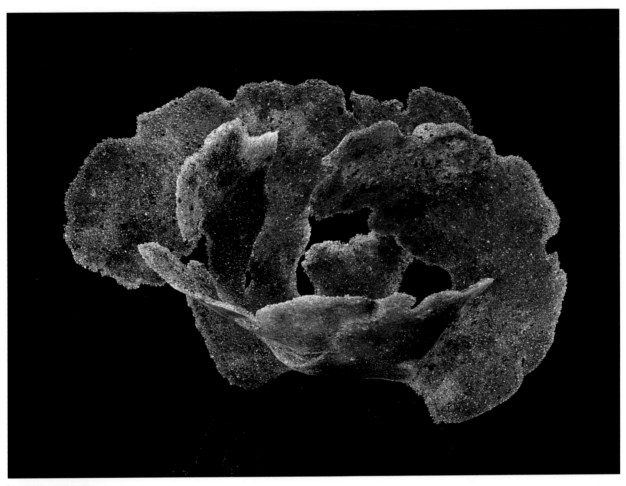

JANET KELMAN
Blue-Green Sea Gem, 2004

9 x 13 x 10 inches (22.9 x 33 x 25.4 cm)

Fritted glass; fused, slumped

Photo by Leslie Patron

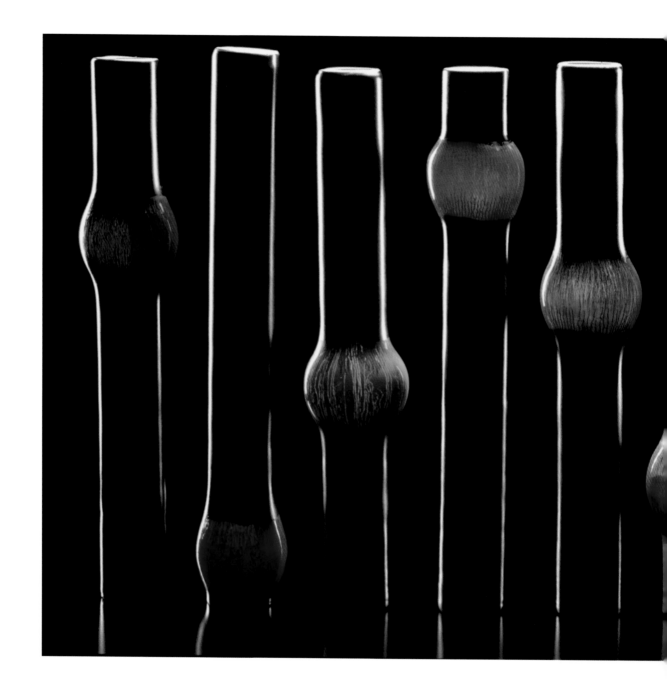

WAMB.
Wamb., 2003

23⅝ x 4 x 4 inches (60 x 10 x 10 cm)

Blown glass, paint; cold worked

Collaborative work

Photo by Grant Hancock

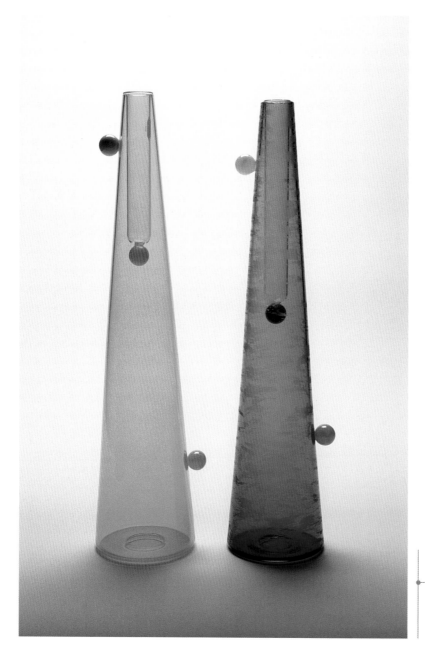

TAKUYA TOKIZAWA
Cone Bud Vases, 2003

15 x 4½ x 4 inches (38.1 x 11.4 x 10.2 cm)
Blown glass; hot worked, etched
Photo by Claire Garoutte

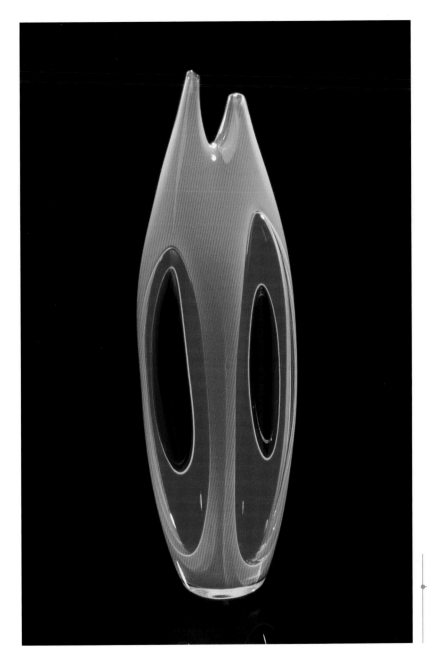

BENJAMIN W. COBB
Double-Neck Window Vase, 2004

20 x 6 x 6 inches (50.8 x 15.2 x 15.2 cm)

Blown glass

Photo by Scott Mitchell Leen

273

M. SEAN MERCER
TCN-MQ-1-3, 2003

18 x 8 x 8 inches (45.7 x 20.3 x 20.3 cm)

Glass, wood, steel, brass

Photo by Eva Heyd

SCOTT F. SCHROEDER
Brookwood, 2004

18 x 4½ x 2½ inches (45.7 x 11.4 x 6.4 cm)

Kiln-cast glass

Photo by Bill Bachhuber

STEVE KLEIN
Lybster III, 2005

6 x 19 x 19 inches (15.2 x 48.3 x 48.3 cm)
Kiln-formed, blown glass
Photo by Jason Van Fleet

RICHARD M. PARRISH
Green & Blue Ginkgo Tray, 2004

2 x 16 x 16 inches (5.1 x 40.6 x 40.6 cm)

Kiln-formed glass, ginkgo leaves; fused, slumped

Photo by Tom Ferris

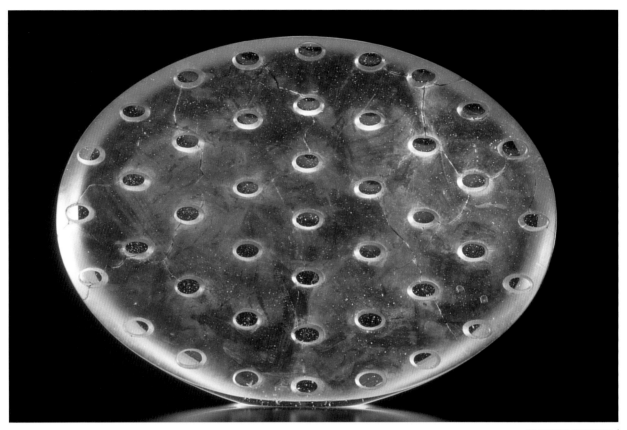

MAYUMI MIYAKE
Mirror, 2004

22¹⁄₁₆ x 28³⁄₈ x 4¾ inches (56 x 72 x 12 cm)

Kiln-cast glass, glue; cold worked

Photo by artist

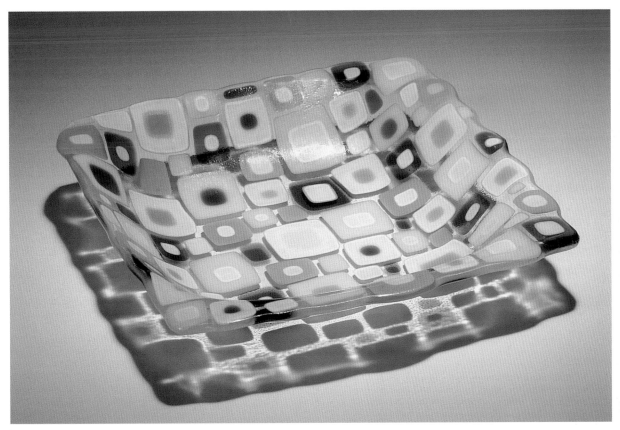

ANGELA SAMPLE
Lounge Around, 2005

2 x 9 x 8 inches (5.1 x 22.9 x 20.3 cm)

Fused, slumped

Photo by Luettke Studio

ROBERT W. STEPHAN
Monolithic Nebulosity, 1999

10¾ x 6³⁄₁₆ x 2⅜ inches
(27.3 x 15.7 x 6.1 cm)

Lead crystal, soda-lime crystal,
dichroic-optical coatings, granite;
laminated, polished

Photos by Mark Bolick

BONTRIDDER THIERRY
Les Ailes du Désir, 1991

27⁹⁄₁₆ x 19¾ x 16½ inches
(70 x 50 x 42 cm)

Laboratory glass, copper, steel

Photo by Paul Louis

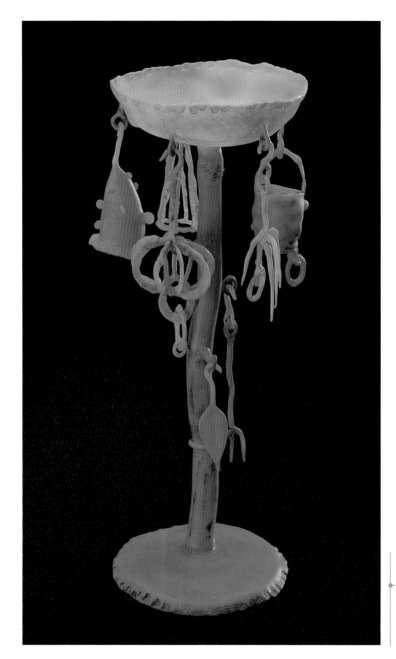

JAY MUSLER
Charmed, 2004

9¼ x 4½ x 4½ inches (23.5 x 11.4 x 11.4 cm)

Lampworked glass; sandblasted, oil painted

Photo by Sibila Savage

STEPHAN COX
Ruby and Green Floral, 2005

42 x 15 x 15 inches (106.7 x 38.1 x 38.1 cm)

Hand-blown, hand-carved glass; cold fused

Photo by Don Pitlik

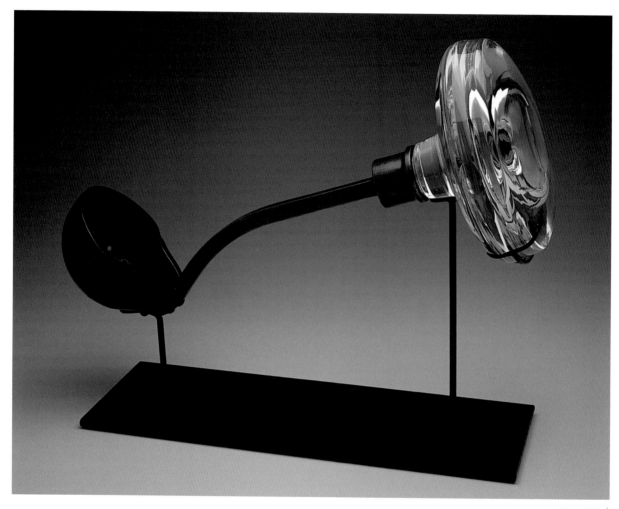

LOU LYNN
Ladle, 2004

20 x 27 x 10 inches (50.8 x 68.6 x 25.4 cm)

Blown glass, bronze

Photo by Janet Dwyer

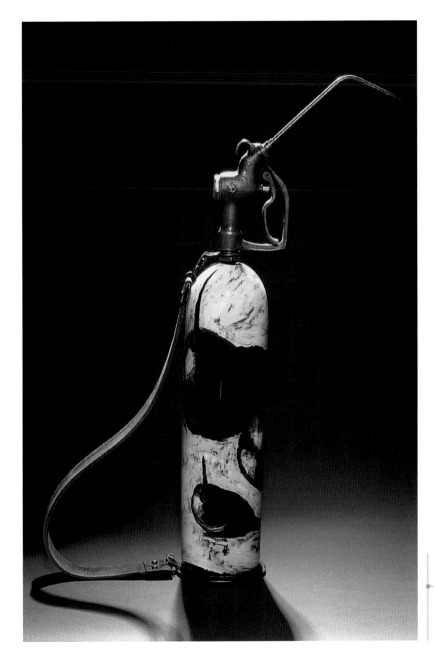

MAGAN STEVENS
Oilcan Series, 2000

24 x 6½ x 6½ inches (61 x 16.5 x 16.5 cm)

Blown glass, mixed media; reverse painted

Photo by Pat Simone

285

FLO PERKINS
Dry Land, 2004

8½ x 7 x 6¾ inches (21.6 x 17.8 x 17.1 cm)
Blown glass, rock
Photo by Addison Doty

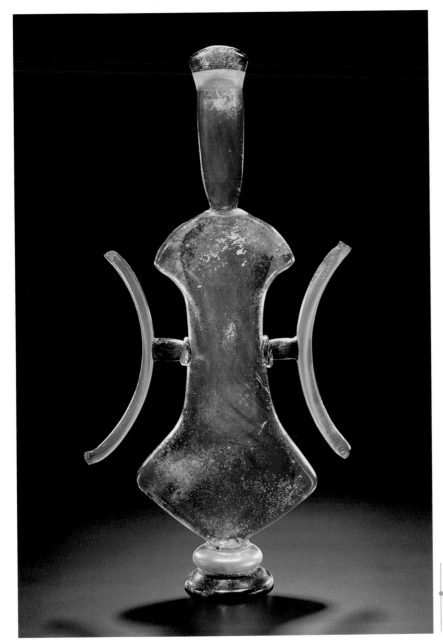

LOUIS SCLAFANI
Bottle Series, 1996

Hot-sculpted glass

Photo by Alex Casler

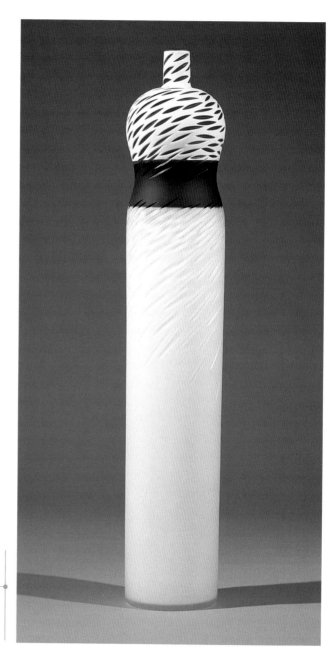

JANE BRUCE
White Sentinel, 2004

31 x 5¼ x 5¼ inches (78.7 x 13.3 x 13.3 cm)

Blown glass; wheel cut, hand finished

Photo by David Paterson

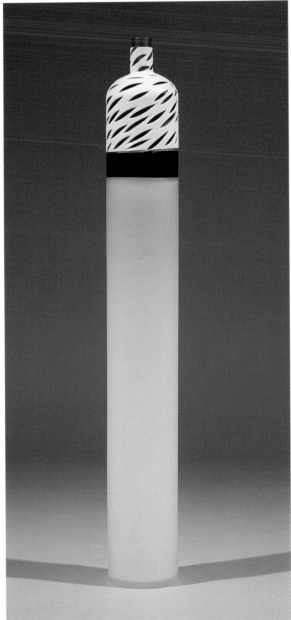

JANE BRUCE
ABOVE

Black/Clear Sentinel, 2003

29 x 6¼ x 6¼ inches (73.7 x 15.9 x 15.9 cm)
Blown glass; wheel cut, hand finished
Photo by David Paterson

LEFT

Primrose Sentinel, 2003

32¼ x 4½ x 4½ inches (81.9 x 11.4 x 11.4 cm)
Blown glass; wheel cut, hand finished
Photo by David Paterson

ELIZABETH RYLAND MEARS
*Shelter Series: Shelter for Protection
of Her Inner World,* 2004

26 x 14 x 14 inches (66 x 35.6 x 35.6 cm)

Glass, lusters, copper, mica, quartz,
wool, horsehair, waxed linen;
planeworked, sandblasted

Photo by Tommy Elder

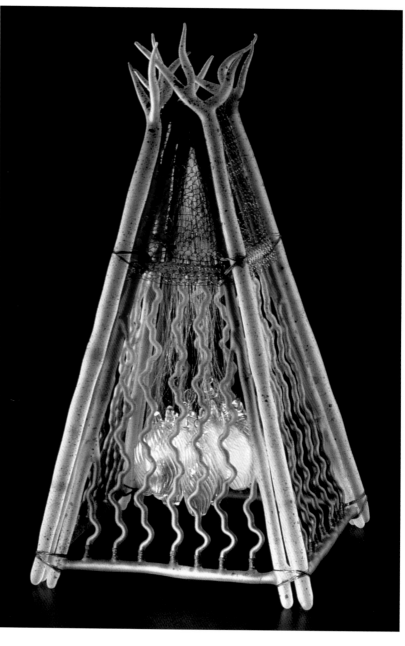

BRENT KEE YOUNG
Fossil Series: Centered, 2003

16 x 9 x 9 inches
(40.6 x 22.9 x 22.9 cm)

Blown glass; graal technique, engraved, negative-relief interior impressions

Photo by Dan Fox / Lumina

291

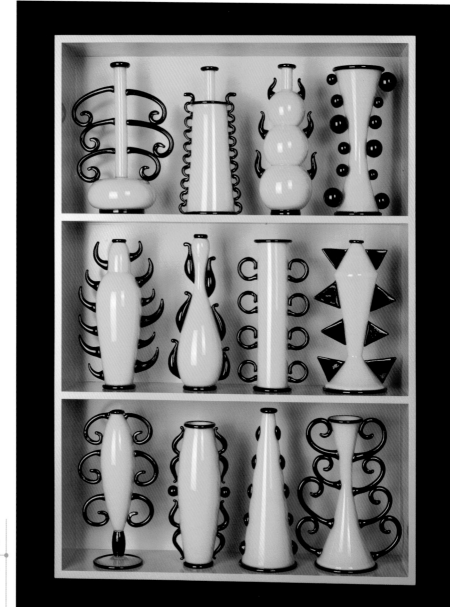

DANTE MARIONI
Yellow Vessel Display, 2004

27 x 19 x 5 inches
(68.6 x 48.3 x 12.7 cm)

Blown glass, wood

Photo by Roger Schreiber

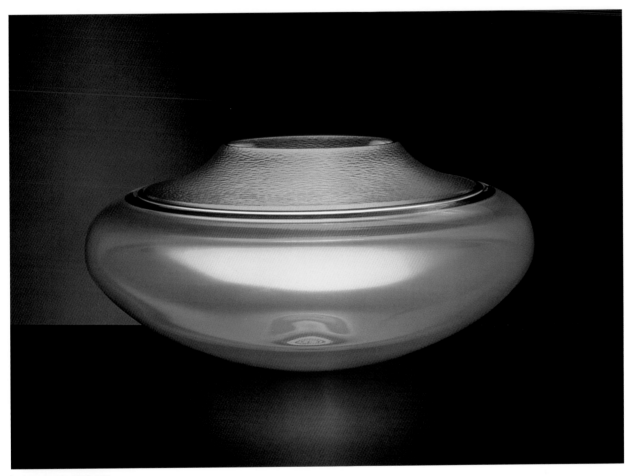

SONJA BLOMDAHL
Citrus/Amber B6902, 2002

6¼ x 12 inches (15.9 x 30.5 cm)

Blown glass; incalmo, battuto

Photo by Lynn Thompson

Even bracelets are possible from this
fire-formed liquid called glass that looks so
delicate, yet has such tremendous strength.

ANN MILLER
Knitght Twist, 2004

3 x 3½ x ¼ inches (7.6 x 8.9 x 3.2 cm)
Borosilicate glass; torch worked, stained
Photo by Jacques Cressaty

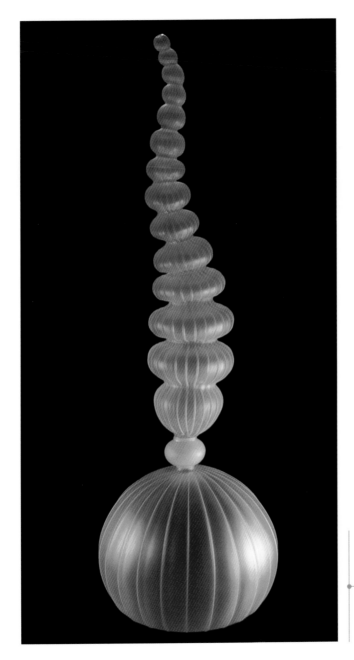

JAY MACDONELL

*Formulations
(Tangerine orange/orange
cane/tangerine orange)*, 2005

33 x 10 x 10 inches (83.8 x 25.4 x 25.4 cm)

Blown glass; joined hot, cane, frosted

Photo by artist

WENDY HANNAM
City Limit #3, 2003

11 x 11 x 3½ inches (28 x 28 x 9 cm)

Hand-blown glass; color overlay,
sandblasted, engraved

Photo by Grant Hancock

JUDITH LA SCOLA
Ivy, 2004

18 x 13 x 10 inches (45.7 x 33 x 25.4 cm)

Plate, blown, and cast glass, copper base; sandblasted, painted, etched

Photos by Rob Vinnedge

297

COLIN REID
#R870, 1999

9½ x 17 x 17 inches (24 x 43 x 43 cm)

Kiln-cast optical glass

Photo by artist

BANDHU SCOTT DUNHAM
Blue Basket, 2004

7 x 11 x 11 inches (17.8 x 27.9 x 27.9 cm)

Borosilicate glass; lampworked,
sandblasted, lustered

Photo by artist

My favorite part of making

objects is improvising.

JAY MUSLER
Slinky, 2003

8½ x 9 x 3½ inches
(21.6 x 22.9 x 8.9 cm)

Lampworked glass;
sandblasted, oil painted

Photo by Sibila Savage

DAN DAILEY
Female Alligator, 1998

20½ x 11 x 8½ inches
(52.1 x 27.9 x 21.6 cm)

Hand-blown glass, iron-oxide
crackle; sandblasted, acid-polished

Photo by Bill Truslow

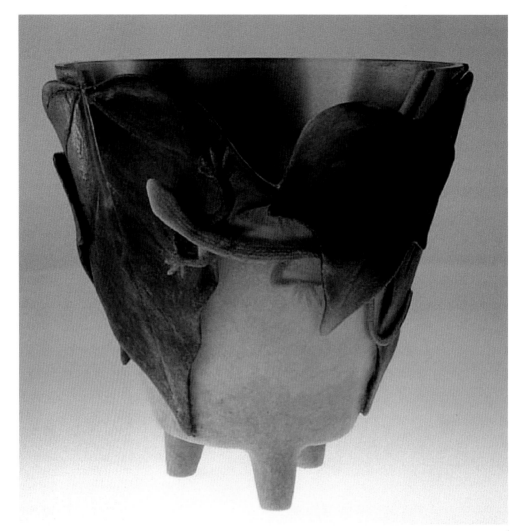

ELLEN ABBOTT
MARC LEVA
Hunting Ground, 2004

6½ x 6½ x 6½ inches
(16.5 x 16.5 x 16.5 cm)

Kiln-cast glass; pâte de verre, cold worked

Photo by artist

MARK PEISER
Oasis, 1979

5⅝ x 4⁹⁄₁₆ x 4⁹⁄₁₆ inches
(14.3 x 11.6 x 11.6 cm)

Blown glass; layered, torchworked imagery

Photo by Ann Hawthorne

JOSH SIMPSON
Inhabited Vase, 2003

7 x 5 x 5 inches (17.5 x 12.7 x 12.7 cm)

Blown glass; multi-layered, filigrana cane
inclusions, precious metals

Photo by Tommy Olof Elder

PAUL J. STANKARD
Damselfly Over Tea Roses, Blueberries, and Bulbous Roots Botanical, 2003

5½ inches high (14 cm)

Flameworked glass

Photo by Douglas Schaible

SUSAN J. LONGINI
Amphora: Pumpkin/Mauve, 2003

18 x 15 x 5 inches
(45.7 x 38.1 x 12.7 cm)

Pâte de verre glass, reservoir-cast
base; assembled

Photo by Bullseye Glass Company

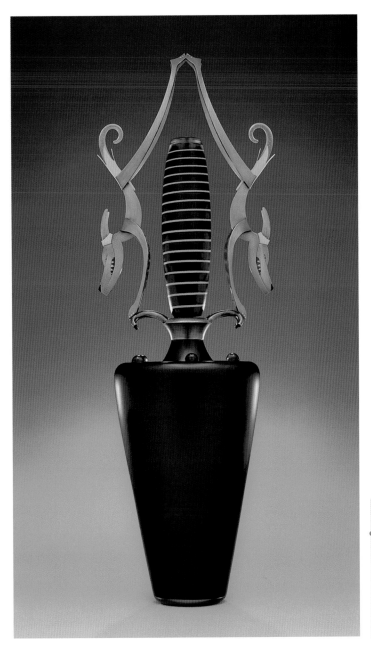

DAN DAILEY
Double Dogs, 2004

25¼ x 8½ x 7 inches
(64.1 x 21.6 x 17.8 cm)

Hand-blown glass, sandblasted,
acid-polished, fabricated, patinated,
nickel- and gold-plated bronze; pâte de
verre, vitrolite and lampworked details

Photo by Bill Truslow

I wanted to capture the energy of water. It can
be calming and yet powerful at the same time.

JENNIFER SMITH
Water Bowl Set, 2002

4 x 17 x 14 inches (10.2 x 43.2 x 35.6 cm)
Cast glass; sandblasted
Photo by artist

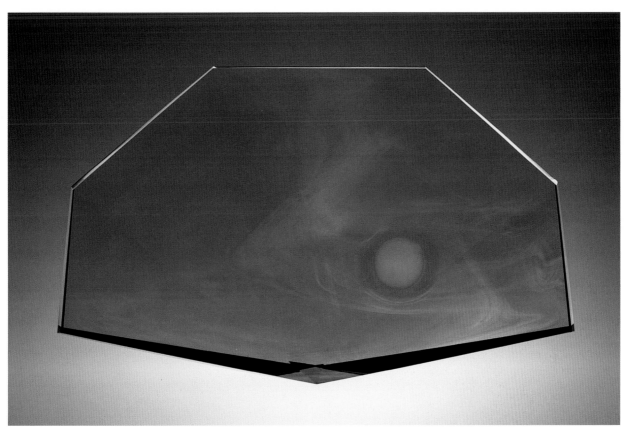

MARK PEISER
What Time Is It, 1983–1994

8¾ x 15⅞ x 2½ inches (22.2 x 40.3 x 6.4 cm)

Compound, cast glass; cut, polished

Photo by artist

GARY BEECHAM
Blue Shift X, 2004

24¾ x 22¾ x 5¼ inches
(62.9 x 57.8 x 13.3 cm)

Glass, stainless steel armature;
fused crystal, color-overlay rods

Photo by John Littleton

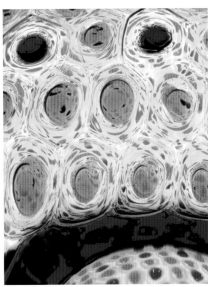

STEPHEN ROLFE POWELL
Burning Manic Scooper, 2004

28 x 23 x 19¼ inches (71.1 x 58.4 x 48.9 cm)

Blown glass; murrini surface

Assisted by Chris Bohach, Jon Capps, Matt Cummings, Paul Hugues, and Ted Jeckering

Photos by David Harpe

ANNE ELISE PEMBERTON
Microcosm I, 2005

18½ x 16 x 4½ inches
(47 x 40.6 x 11.4 cm)

Sheet glass, maple shadow box,
recessed backlighting, multi-layered
panels; pâte de verre, laminated,
cold worked

Photos by Mark Gulezian

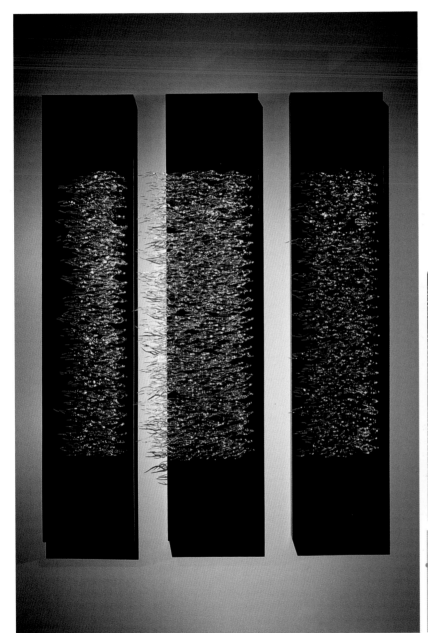

SUSAN EDGERLEY
Gust Triptych: Seed Saver Series, 2004

66 x 52 x 5 inches
(167.6 x 132.1 x 12.7 cm)

Flameworked glass, wood

Photos by Michel Dubreuil

BRIAN F. RUSSELL
Hemisphere 44 Valentine, 2005

20 x 20 x 17 inches (50.8 x 50.8 x 43.2 cm)

Cast glass, forged steel

Photo by artist

MARK PEISER
Contrition Second Study, 2003

7 x 6½ x 6½ inches
(17.8 x 16.5 x 16.5 cm)

Cast opal glass; hand finished,
sandblasted, acid polished

Photo by Douglas Schaible

In this piece I took a closer look at how flowers were used to decorate table centers in the nineteenth century. I was exploring the contemporary form of a historic idea.

SUSAN RANKIN
Epergne: Purple Scroll, 2003

20⅞ x 9½ x 4¹⁵⁄₁₆ inches
(53 x 24 x 12.5 cm)

Blown glass, solid-worked glass; sandblasted, assembled

Photo by Trent Photographic

KURT SWANSON
LISA SCHWARTZ
Jeweltone Ursulabras, 2004

14 x 8 x 4 inches (35.6 x 20.3 x 10.2 cm)

Solid and blown glass

Photo by Bob Barrett

DAVID JAMES
Rustica, 2002

10 x 15⅕ x 6 inches
(25.4 x 38.6 x 15.2 cm)

Lead crystal; pâte de verre, lost wax

Photo by André Cornellier

This could be an artifact from a dinner table, discovered in an archeological dig somewhere in the eastern Mediterranean.

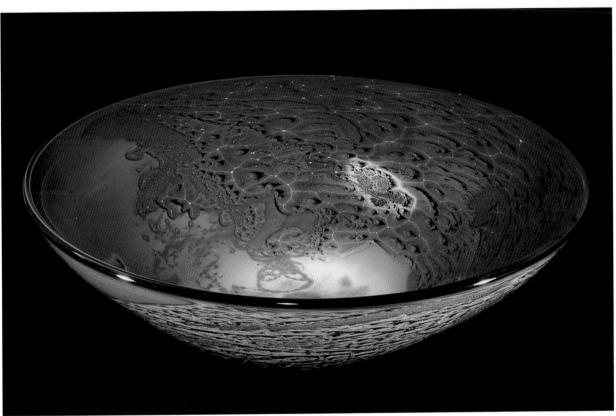

JOSH SIMPSON
Blue New Mexico Bowl, 1998

6 x 20 x 20 inches (15.2 x 50.8 x 50.8 cm)

Blown glass; hand formed,
reactive silver decoration

Photo by Tommy Olof Elder

Most of my work reflects
a compromise between the
glass and me. The piece is
finished when we both agree.

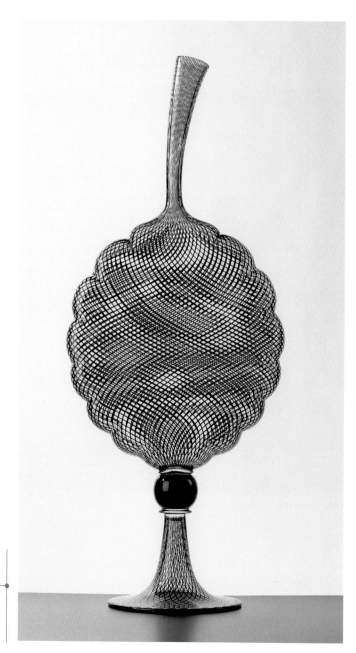

DANTE MARIONI
Black Reticello Leaf, 2004

26 x 11 inches (66 x 27.9 cm)
Blown glass
Photo by Roger Schreiber

JASON RUFF
Medusa, 2004

21 x 28 x 25 inches (53.3 x 71.1 x 63.5 cm)

Hand-blown glass; solid, hot-sculpted
exterior bit work

Photo by artist

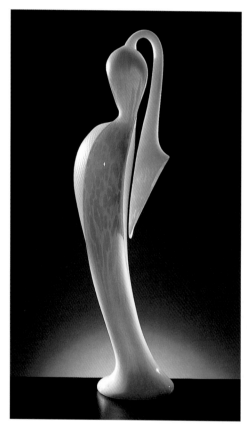

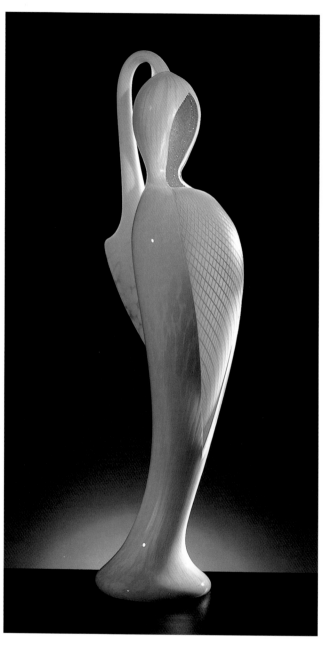

JANUSZ POŹNIAK
Grace, 2002

26 x 7 x 7 inches (66 x 17.8 x 17.8 cm)

Blown glass; multi-layered, reticello,
sandblasted, cut, polished

Photos by Russell Johnson

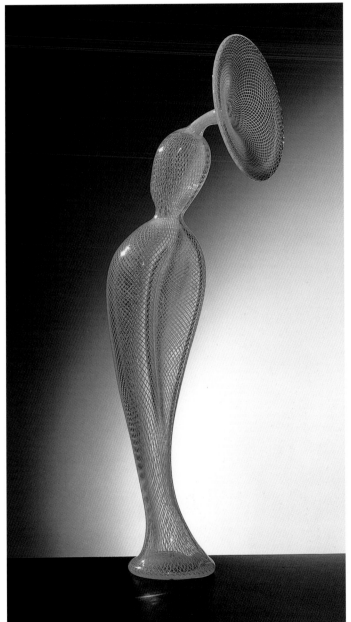

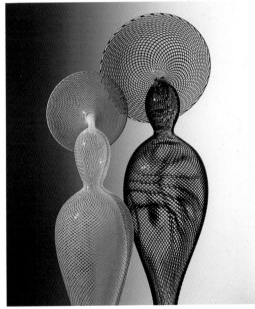

JANUSZ POŹNIAK
Halcyon, 2002

32 x 8 x 9 inches (81.3 x 20.3 x 22.9 cm)

Blown glass; assembled

Photos by Russell Johnson

323

JAMES MINSON
Blue-Ringed Octopus Chandelier, 2004

24 x 30 x 24 inches (61 x 76.2 x 61 cm)

Flameworked glass

Photo by artist

JANET KELMAN
Fuchsia in Bloom, 2004

9¾ x 20 x 18 inches (24.8 x 50.8 x 45.7 cm)

Blown glass; sandblasted, slumped

Photo by Leslie Patron

ELLEN ABBOTT
MARC LEVA
Honey Cup, 2003

4 x 3½ x 3½ inches
(10.2 x 8.9 x 8.9 cm)

Kiln-cast glass; pâte de verre,
cold worked

Photo by Greg Kolanowski

ELLEN ABBOTT
MARC LEVA
Dreamer Series: Vision Quest, 2004

4½ x 9½ x 9½ inches (11.4 x 24.1 x 24.1 cm)

Kiln-cast glass; pâte de verre, cold worked

Photo by artist

DAVID SCHNUCKEL
Geseundheit Series, 2002

Tallest: 13¾ inches (34.9 cm)
Blown glass
Photo by George Abiad

FRITZ DREISBACH
Grape and Scallop Goblets, 1992

Tallest: 14½ inches (35.6 cm)

Glass

Photo by artist

BRIAN F. RUSSELL
Bounce, 2005

34 x 23 x 11 inches
(86.4 x 58.4 x 27.9 cm)

Cast glass, forged bronze

Photo by artist

Fish have to carry on swimming to stay alive. I feel that is common in my life too. Ever since I realized that, I have put fish in my work.

HIROSHI YAMANO
From East to West: Fish Catcher #110, 2002

15¾ x 14⁹⁄₁₆ x 14⁹⁄₁₆ inches
(40 x 37 x 37 cm)

Blown and sculpted glass; cut, polished, silver-leaf engraved, electroplated

Photo by artist

DANTE MARIONI
Blue Trio, 2004

Tallest: 29 inches (73.7 cm)
Blown glass
Photo by Roger Schreiber

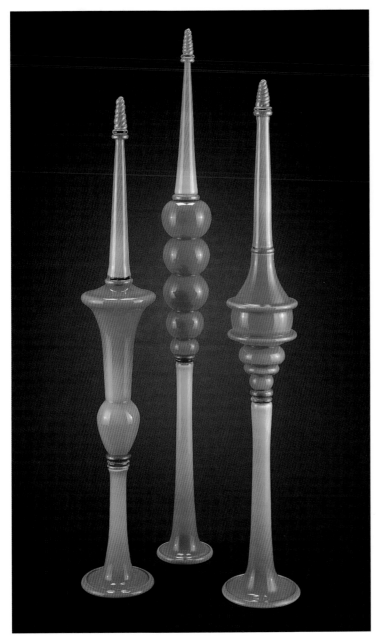

These improbable architectural forms with stoppers are intended to express dignity and grace while uplifting the viewer through the use of form, light, and color.

RANDY MYERS
Luminosity, 2004

41 x 22 x 10 inches (104.1 x 55.9 x 25.4 cm)
Blown glass
Photo by Rob Vinnedge

MARY VAN CLINE
The Receding Nature of Time, 2000

15 x 24 x 6 inches (38.1 x 61 x 15.2 cm)

Photo-sensitive glass; pâte de verre

Photo by Rob Vinnedge

HIROSHI YAMANO
From East to West:
Fish Hanger #21, 2003

39⅜ x 12¾ x 5 inches
(100 x 32 x 12.5 cm)

Blown glass; cut, polished,
engraved, electroplated

Photo by Yoichi Kimura

335

SUSAN EDGERLEY
Threadlet on a Filament, 2003

15 x 5 inches (38.1 x 12.7 cm)
Flameworked blown glass, metal
Photo by Michel Dubreuil

BETH HYLEN
Frozen Spring, 2001

7¹⁄₁₆ x 7⁷⁄₈ inches (18 x 20 cm)

Borosilicate glass, sterling silver snake chain;
lampworked, sandblasted, silver-leaf gilded

Photo by Dan Neuberger

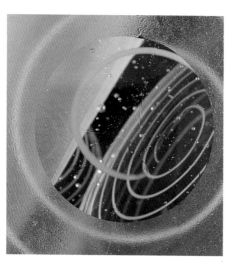

GARY BOLT
Armillary Sphere #2, 2004

14 x 12 x 12 inches (35.6 x 30.5 x 30.5 cm)

Sandcast glass, hot-worked inclusions,
welded-steel base; cut, ground, polished

Photos by Vince Klassen

MICHÈLE LAPOINTE
*Comme une Rivierè Qui Transperce
la Ville (Like a River That Ran Through
the City)*, 2002

47¼ x 25⁹⁄₁₆ x 15¾ inches each
(120 x 65 x 40 cm)

Blown glass, molded clay, computerized map,
historical texts on Canal Lachine

Photo by Michel Dubreuil

PENELOPE WURR
Oval Patchwork Botanical Vase, 2003

8 x 5 x 3 inches each (20.3 x 12.7 x 7.6 cm)

Mold-blown glass; translucent enamel overlay

Photo by artist

MARK SUDDUTH
Canted Pair, 2004

12 x 10 x 10 inches each (30.5 x 25.4 x 25.4 cm)

Hand-blown glass; cut, polished, engraved

Photo by artist

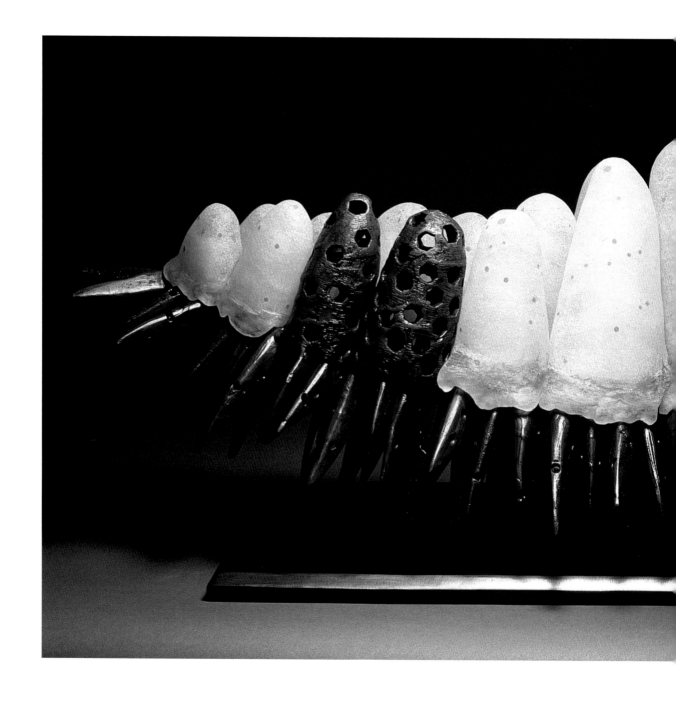

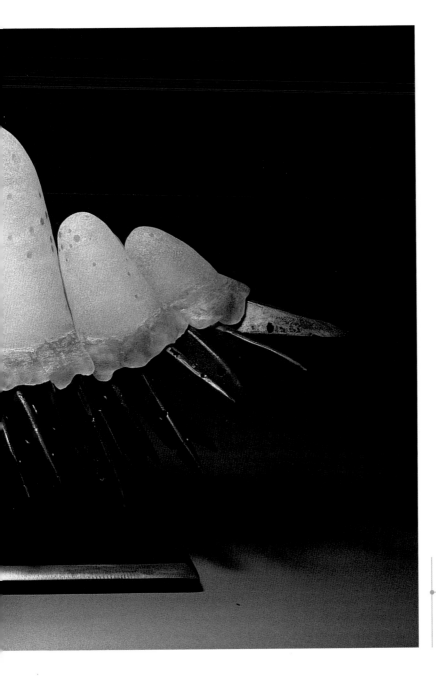

MASAMI KODA
Green Sprinkle, 2004

11 x 26 x 9 inches (27.9 x 66 x 22.9 cm)

Cast glass, bronze, steel

Photo by artist

JAMES MINSON
Jellyfish Chandelier, 2004

40 x 36 x 40 inches (101.6 x 91.4 x 101.6 cm)

Flameworked glass

Photo by artist

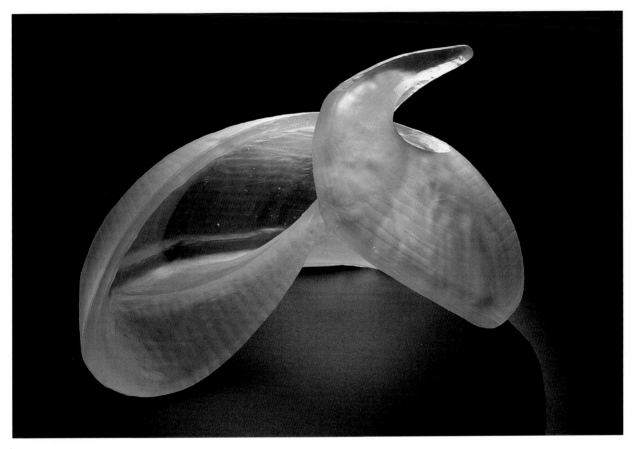

DONALD ROBERTSON
Volute, 2003

8½ x 13 x 10 inches (21.6 x 33 x 25.4 cm)

Crystal, wood; lost-wax cast, cut, polished

Photo by Michel Dubreuil

DEBORAH HORRELL
Still Life—Still, 2003

14⅝ x 18½ x 6¾ inches (37.2 x 47 x 17.1 cm)

Cast glass; hollow pâte de verre, solid cast

Photo by Paul Foster

KAIT RHOADS
Pinstripe, 2004

15½ x 6½ x 6½ inches (39.4 x 16.5 x 16.5 cm)

Blown glass; cane, vein murrine

Photo by Roger Schreiber

MIKE PENFOUND
Alien Vacation, 2004

4½ x 3½ x 3½ inches (11.4 x 8.9 x 8.9 cm)

Blown glass; sandblasted, reheated, shaped

Photos by artist

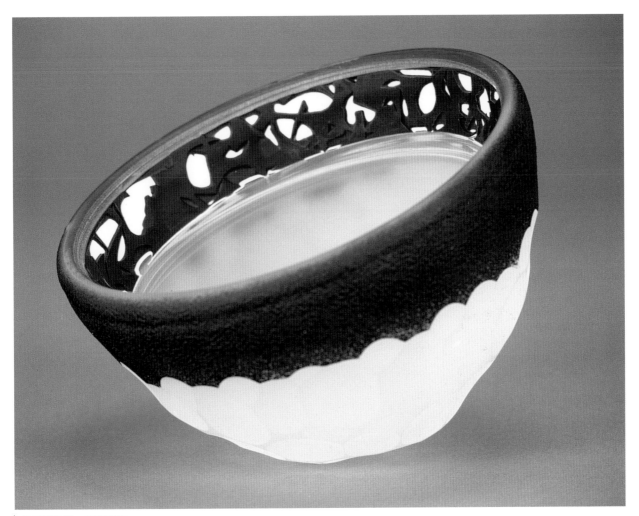

DAMON MacNAUGHT
Carved Bowl, 2003

7 x 7 x 7 inches (17.8 x 17.8 x 17.8 cm)

Blown glass; incalmo, sandblasted,
acid etched, wheel cut

Photo by John Lucas

JOYCE J. SCOTT
If Life Were A Tree, 2003

27 x 18 x 13 inches (68.6 x 45.7 x 33 cm)

Blown, slumped, lampworked glass,
peyote stitched beads, mixed-media

Photo by artist

DICK MARQUIS
Marquiscarpa #2000-6, 2000

5 x 4¼ x 3½ inches (12.7 x 10.8 x 8.9 cm)

Wheel-carved glass; fused, slumped, and blown, murrine technique

Photo by artist

351

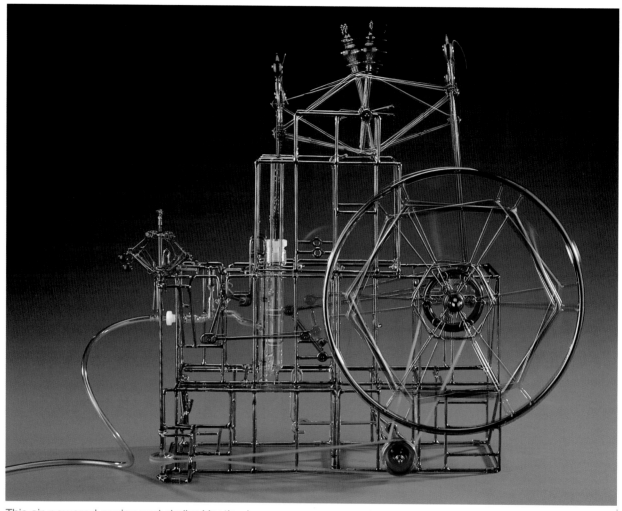

This air-powered engine and similar kinetic pieces represent a full turn of the circle, re-enlivening the playfully scientific attitude that brought me to glasswork in the first place. I have finally gotten my wish to be a mad scientist.

BANDHU SCOTT DUNHAM
Kinetic Engine #3, 2004

36 x 36 x 10 inches (91.4 x 91.4 x 25.4 cm)

Borosilicate glass, teflon, rubber; lampworked, lustered

Photo by Christopher Marchetti

JOEL PHILIP MYERS
Canvas #9, 2003

15 x 6 x 6 inches
(38.1 x 15.2 x 15.2 cm)

Mold-blown glass, glass ice,
enamel

Photo by John Herr

JAY MUSLER
Picking, 2004

10 x 6 x 4 inches (25.4 x 15.2 x 10.2 cm)

Lampworked glass; sandblasted,
oil painted

Photo by Sibila Savage

JOYCE J. SCOTT
Yellow-Faced, Lizard-Ridden, Splint-Legged Jar Woman #10, 2003

29 x 9 x 22 inches (73.7 x 22.9 x 55.9 cm)

Glass jars, peyote stitched beads, African wood sculpture

Photo by artist

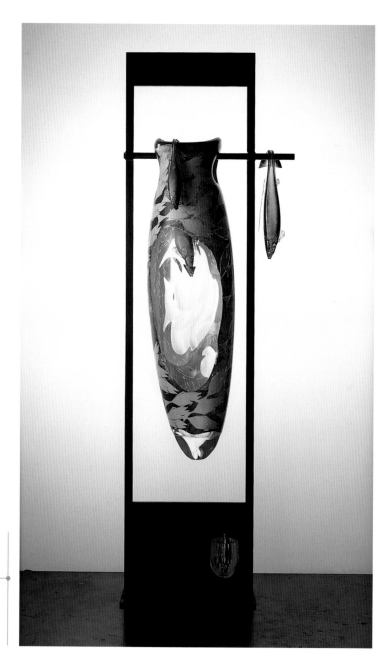

HIROSHI YAMANO
From East to West:
Fish Hanger #39, 2003

63 x 15¾ x 11¾ inches (160 x 40 x 30 cm)

Blown glass; cut, polished,
engraved, electroplated

Photo by Yoichi Kimura

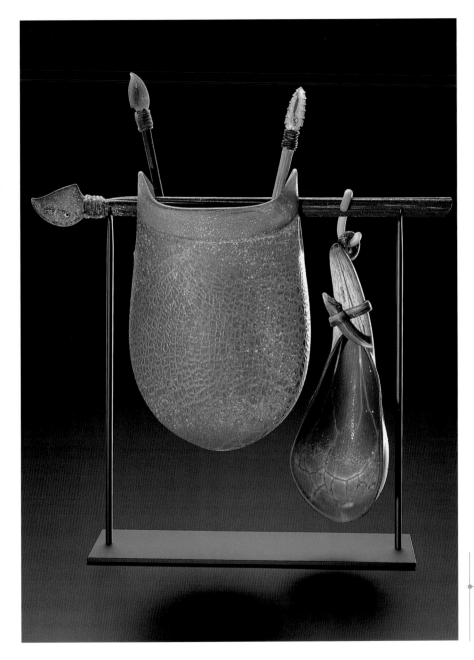

WILLIAM MORRIS
Suspended Artifact, 1995

27 x 24 x 5 inches (68.6 x 61 x 12.7 cm)

Blown and sculpted glass, steel stand

Photo by Rob Vinnedge

357

GABRIELE KÜSTNER
Untitled, 2003

9½ x 5¾ inches diameter (24 x 14.5 cm)

Blown glass, silicone-applied glass cane;
cold worked, battuto ground

Photo by Maxwell

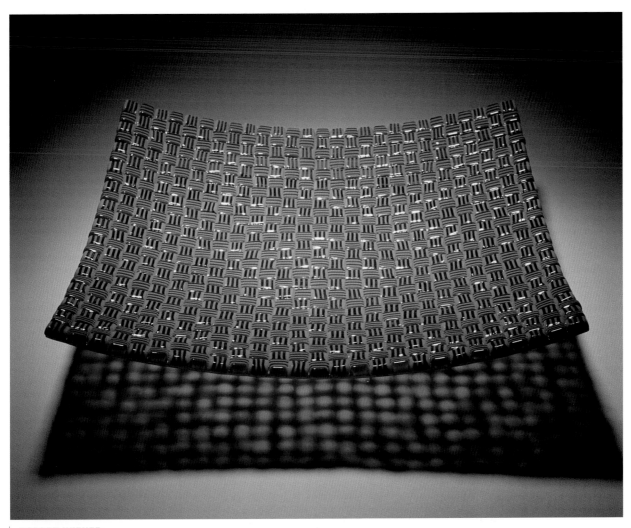

ROBERT WIENER
Key Lime, 2004

15 x 15 inches (38.1 x 38.1 cm)

Fused glass; cold worked, slumped

Photo by Pete and Alison Duvall

FRITZ DREISBACH
*Opaline Cantelope Mongo Urn with Optical
Spirals and Wavy, Wet Foot Base,* 1994

13½ x 19 x 17 inches (34.3 x 48.3 x 43.2 cm)

Glass

Photo by artist

LESLIE PATRON
Untitled, 2003

7 x 12 inches (17.8 x 30.5 cm)

Blown glass; sandblasted

Photo by Leslie Patron

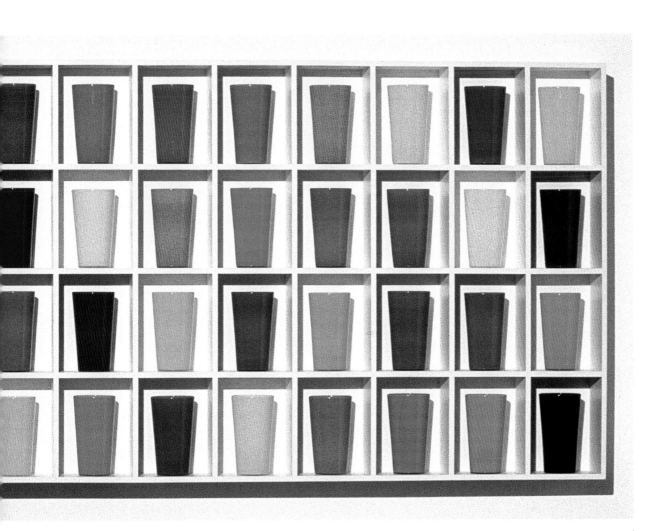

SEAN ALBERT
The Phenomenon of Light (Tumblers), 2004

28 x 90 x 5 inches (71.1 x 228.6 x 12.7 cm)

Blown glass, wood, paint

Photo by Russell Johnson

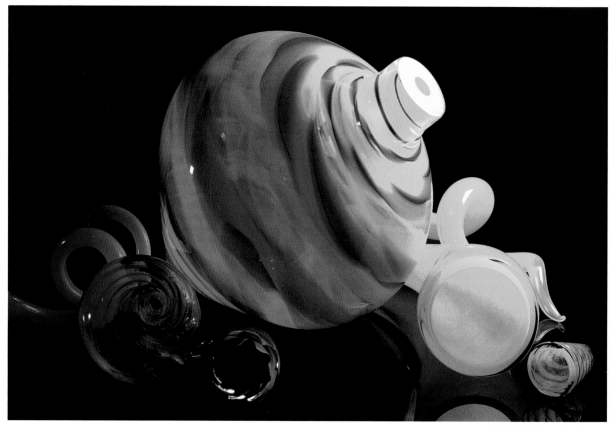

KATHLEEN MULCAHY
Golden Spinner Group, 2000

21 x 30 x 24 inches (53.3 x 76.2 x 61 cm)

Blown glass

Photo by artist

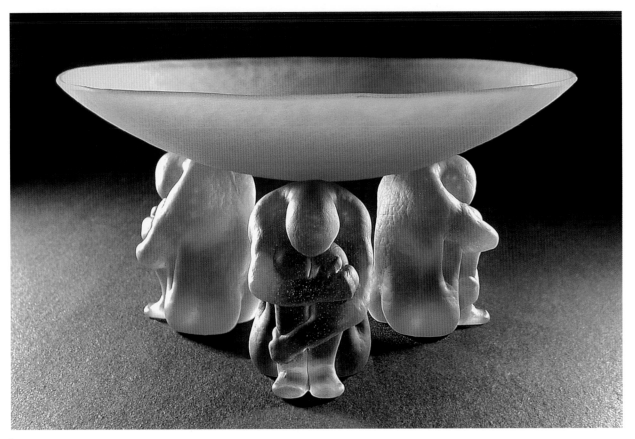

JENNIFER SMITH
Sittiein with Bowl, 2002

7½ x 14 inches diameter (19 x 35.6 cm)

Cast glass; sandblasted

Photo by artist

SCOTT F. SCHROEDER
Hope, 2004

30½ x 6⅝ x 4¾ inches
(77.5 x 17 x 12 cm)

Kiln-cast glass

Photo by Bill Bachhuber

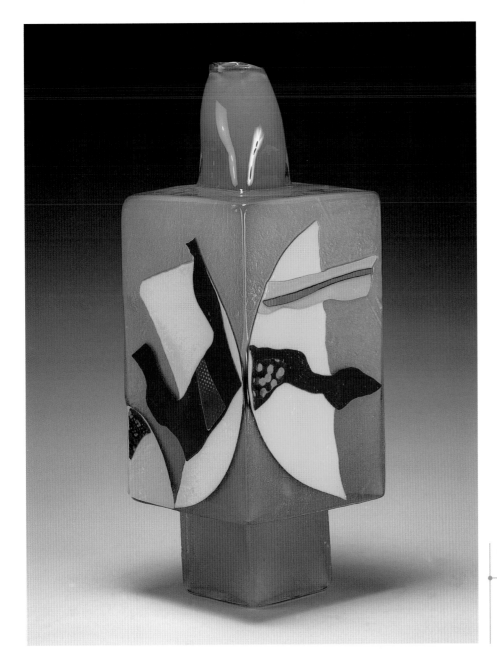

JOEL PHILIP MYERS
Canvas #13, 2004

17 x 6 x 6 inches
(43.2 x 15.2 x 15.2 cm)

Mold-blown glass; sharded

Photo by John Herr

Even as a child, I felt ancient vessels, though often imperfectly reassembled, were much more interesting than slick, perfect pieces. In creating my own vessels with glass powders and frits, I reference classical forms, beauty vs. perfection, and the vessel as a receptacle for our aspirations.

SUSAN J. LONGINI
Vase Analogy: Pumpkin/Mauve, 2001

11 x 12 x 6 inches (27.9 x 30.5 x 15.2 cm)

Pâte de verre glass, reservoir-cast base; assembled

Photo by artist

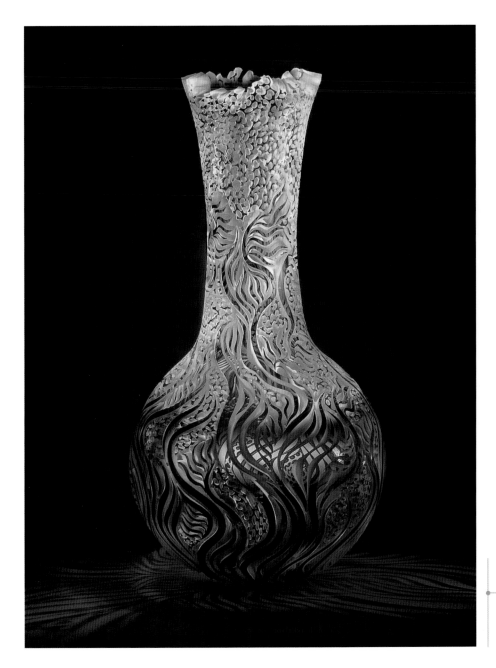

DEBRA MAY
Embellished Cantarrito, 2004

18 x 8 inches (45.7 x 20.3 cm)

Blown glass; sandblasted

Photo by Robin Stancliff

ANDREW WU
Cheryl, 2004

7 x 9 x 9 inches (17.8 x 22.9 x 22.9 cm)
Blown glass; multi-layered, sandblasted
Photo by artist

DANIELLE BLADE
STEPHEN GARTNER
*Strata Covered Bowl with Bone and
Tendril Finial*, 2003

14 x 9 x 14 inches (35.6 x 22.9 x 35.6 cm)

Blown, hot sculpted glass

Photo by Jonathan Wallen

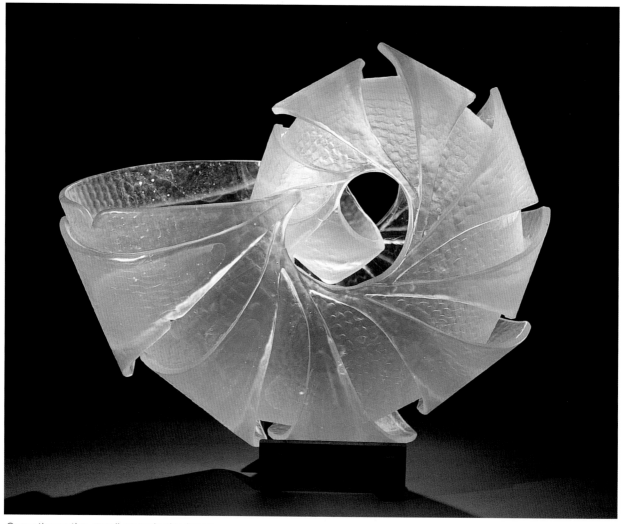

Sometimes the small reveals the large.
This hollow-cast piece was inspired by
photos of the spiral galaxies.

DONALD ROBERTSON
Large Carapace III, 2004

20 x 16 x 11 inches (50.8 x 40.6 x 27.9 cm)
Crystal, wood; lost-wax cast, cut, polished
Photo by Michel Dubreuil

The chambered or pearly nautilus is a mollusk, a "living fossil" whose close relatives date back hundreds of millions of years into geologic history. The life and habits of the nautilus are, for the most part, a mystery. My glass nautilus is rotated up and flared to become a vessel.

ELIN CHRISTOPHERSON
Nautilus, 2004

7½ x 4½ x 3 inches
(19.1 x 11.4 x 7.6 cm)

Blown and solid glass

Photo by Hans-Jürgen Bergmann

PAUL J. STANKARD
Swarming Honeybee Orb, 2004

5½ inches diameter (14 cm)
Hotworked, flameworked glass
Photo by Douglas Schaible

SUSAN RANKIN
Epergne: Blue with Yellow Flowers, 2003

14 x 13¾ x 13⅜ inches (38 x 35 x 34 cm)

Blown and solid-worked glass, steel, patina; sandblasted, assembled

Photo by Trent Photographic

Glass is so much
like water.

SALLY PRASCH
Splash, 2003

12 x 12 x 12 inches
(30.5 x 30.5 x 30.5 cm)

Flameworked

Photo by Tommy Elder

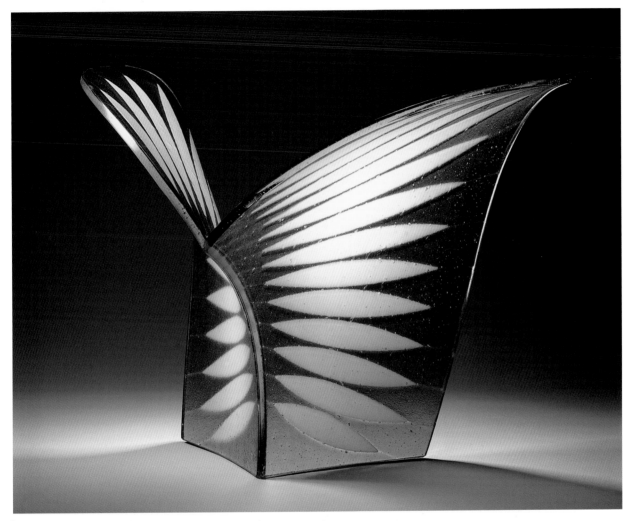

BONTRIDDER THIERRY
Untitled, 2004

19½ x 28½ x 21½ inches (49 x 73 x 55 cm)

Fused, thermoformaged glass

Photo by Paul Louis

377

All of the glass a married couple would need.

KATHERINE GRAY
"For Ever" "And Ever," 2005

Left: 15 inches tall (38.1 cm)
Right: 16 inches tall (40.6 cm)

Blown glass

Photo by Victor Bracke

RIK ALLEN
Azaziel, 2003

36 x 14 x 14 inches
(91.4 x 35.6 x 35.6 cm)

Blown glass, brass, screen, steel wire

Photo by Russell Johnson

JOYCE J. SCOTT
Jarwoman #VI, 1995–1997

14 x 14 x 10 inches
(35.6 x 35.6 x 25.4 cm)

Glass jar, peyote-stitched beads,
bones, crabshells

Photo by artist

I am fascinated with the human figure and like to manipulate the proportions of limbs.

HANS GODO FRÄBEL
Contemplation: Longfellow Series No. 9, 2005

23 inches tall (58.4 cm)

Lampworked glass; sandblasted

Photo by Yasuko Rudisill

My ideas are driven by unconscious thoughts, spontaneous fantasies, and dreams. I have learned to say things and express ideas with glass that I cannot in voice or word, and so my work ends up educating me, as long as I am willing to pay attention.

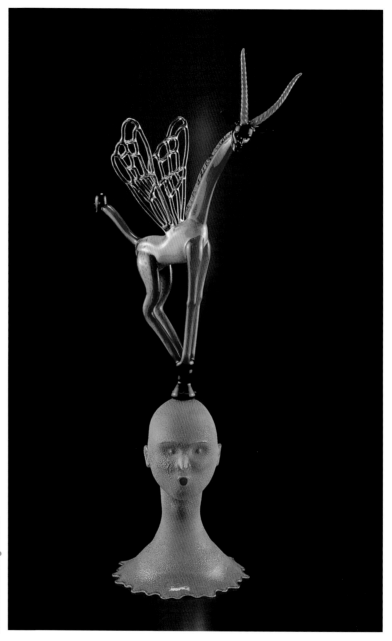

ROBERT A. MICKELSEN
Origin of Dreams, 2004

23½ x 10 x 6 inches
(59.7 x 25.4 x 15.2 cm)

Lampworked glass; assembled, blown, sculpted

Photo by Dan Abbott

This is a peaceful
place for a soul.

CHIHIRO MAKIO
Table Talisman IV, 2000

9 x 4 x 4 inches (22.9 x 10.2 x 10.2 cm)

Cast glass, plate glass, brass, sterling silver;
polished, sandblasted, fabricated

Photo by Ivo M. Vermeulen

This current series of work has been a meditation on the relationship between human and equine. As civilization has been predominantly built on the back of a horse, this creature has played an all-pervasive role in the history of mankind. Its presence is associated with worship and magic and has sometimes reached a divine status.

SHELLEY MUZYLOWSKI ALLEN
Quixote, 2003

28 x 27 x 7 inches
(71.1 x 68.6 x 17.8 cm)

Blown glass, silver foil, horse hair, chain mail, steel stand; hand-sculpted, constructed

HANS GODO FRÄBEL
Jazz Dancers, Dancers Series No. 13, 2003

19 x 25 x 17 inches (48.3 x 63.5 x 43.2 cm)

Lampworked glass; sandblasted

Photo by Yasuko Rudisill

The movement of the dancer intrigues me, especially when dancing to the tunes of jazz musicians.

This piece is about my
socially inept moments,
which I hope to grow out of!

MORNA TUDOR
Social Caterpillar 2, 2001

11 x 5 x 5 inches (27.9 x 12.7 x 12.7 cm)

Blown glass, paint

Photo by Vince Klassen

ANDREW WU
Untitled, 2004

8 x 8 x 8 inches (20.3 x 20.3 x 20.3 cm)

Blown glass; multilayered, sandblasted

Photo by artist

SAM STANG
Reticello Incalmo Bowl, 2003

5½ x 17 inches (14 x 43.2 cm)

Blown glass, reticello center

Photo by Dale Taylor

BRUCE PIZZICHILLO
DARI GORDON

Mosaic Incalmo Bowl, 2005

22 x 22 x 11 inches (55.9 x 55.9 x 27.9 cm)

Blown glass; multi-layered encased decoration;
incalmo technique

Photo by Lee Fatherree

Neon and rolled aluminum tubing wrap upwards around an elevator shaft in a re-modeled shopping plaza in Silver Spring, Maryland.

CRAIG A. KRAFT
Lightweb, 2004

420 x 120 x 120 inches (10.7 x 3.1 x 3.1 m)
Rolled aluminum tubing, neon glass tubing
Photo by artist

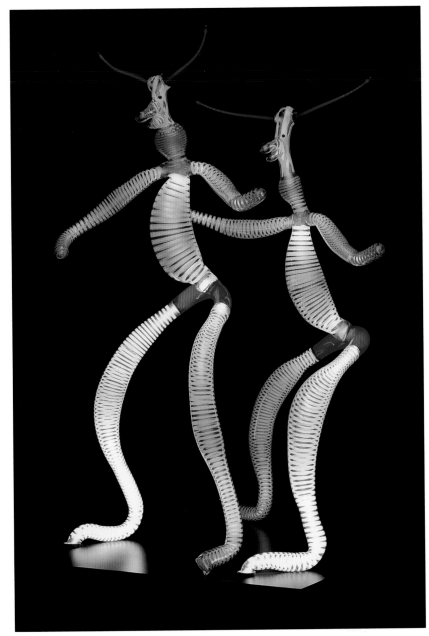

I manipulate the phosphor coatings on the inside of the tubing to create surface designs.

DAVID SVENSON
Two White Long Horn, 1994

22 x 16 x 16 inches (55.9 x 40.6 x 40.6 cm)

Phosphor-coated and colored glass, neon

Photo by Robert Taylor

391

Acknowledgments

To all the many talented artists who submitted images of their work for consideration in this book, our sincere thanks. Your glass creations are truly exciting, and we would not have been able to add a glass book to our 500 series without your interest in sharing your work and artistry with others.

To our juror Maurine Littleton for the insight, diligence, and keen understanding you brought to the jurying process and for giving us a glimpse of your encyclopedic knowledge of glass—a big thank you.

To Stacey, our tireless art director, for the creative talent you brought to the art and production of this book—our first time working together, and I hope not the last—thank you. The book looks great.

My sincere thanks for the editorial assistance provided by Dawn Dillingham, and interns Kelly Johnson, Megan McCarter, Metta Pry, David Squires, and Sue Stigleman. Your attention to so many details helped in so many ways. And, to Rebecca Guthrie who cheerfully took on the proofreading of the copy—many thanks.

And to Carol Taylor, president and publisher of Lark Books, who personally lent a hand in reaching out to glass artists to engage their interest in submitting entries for this book—thank you Carol.

—*Susan Mowery Kieffer, Editor*

About the Juror

Maurine Littleton has been director of the Maurine Littleton Gallery in Washington, D.C., since 1984, exhibiting internationally known glass artists as well as artists in fiber, ceramics, and metal. Her gallery works with private collectors, museum and corporate curators, designers, and the U.S. State Department's Art in Embassies program in developing first-rate glass collections.

Over the years she has juried and curated numerous exhibitions and competitions and has lectured extensively on the subject of contemporary glass in museums across the United States.

She is currently on the board of directors of Creative Glass Center of America at Wheaton Village in Millville, New Jersey. The CGCA awards glass fellowships annually to both professional and emerging glass artists.

Index